MIDLIFE MAVERICKS

Women
reinventing
their lives
in
Mexico

Karen Blue

Universal Publishers/uPUBLISH.com

Published by Universal Publishers/uPUBLISH.com
USA • 2000
Order additional copies at: **www.upublish.com/books/blue.htm**

Author permissions at: mexicoblue@prodigy.com.mx
Website: www.mexioblue.homestead.com

Cover Design by Adelle Morgan-Cordero <imagenmx@prodigy.net.mx>

I gratefully acknowledge the many hours of dedicated copyediting and proofreading by Carol Bee <cbee@saber.net>

ISBN: 1-58112-719-7

Library of Congress Cataloging Card Number: 00-107434

Dedication

This book is dedicated to the memory of my loving sister,
Donna Lynn Handlos

and

to the world's marvelous midlife mavericks

[Fifteen percent of all *Midlife Mavericks* profits
will go to local Lakeside charities.]

Table of Contents

Introduction 1

Part I: Is This All There Is? 5

  1 Opting Out 6
  2 In Search of Me 13
  3 Reflections on a Canvas 20
  4 Mirror! Mirror! 27
  5 Sweet Simplicity 37
  6 The Happy Wanderer 48

Part II: It Ain't Over Till the Fat Lady Sings 59

  7 Another Door Opens 60
  8 Bag and Baggage 69
  9 Life in a Treehouse 78
 10 Stretching the Bucks 88
 11 Sweating Bullets 97
 12 Rambo's Sister 108
 13 From Darkness into Light 119

Part III: Indiana "Joans" 131

 14 The Sky Is Falling! 132
 15 The Fake ID 143
 16 Don't Back Up 151
 17 Dancing Granny 162
 18 The Second Time Around 172
 19 Search for Serenity 181

About the Author 191

Introduction

Whatever you can do or dream you can, begin it.
Boldness has genius, power, and magic in it.
Johann Wolfgang von Goethe

Like so many twists and turns in our lives, change and purpose are often inspired by a single comment, a single question.

I was fifty-two when I moved to Ajijic, a small village on the north shore of Lake Chapala, south of Guadalajara, Mexico. About a year later, I began to write. An elderly blonde lady, with a wide-brimmed red hat, stood up after I had read the first chapter of my first novel at the local writers' group. Her voice quavered. "My dear, have you considered interviewing other women and sharing their stories in your book?"

I hadn't.

At the next writers' meeting, I read a short book proposal for *Midlife Mavericks*. The enthusiasm of the group, both men and women, inspired me. "Based on the feedback you're receiving here," the facilitator said, "I would guess this is a book that needs to be written."

I thanked the audience and asked for names of women who had come to Mexico alone in the second half of their life. I wanted to learn their reasons for leaving home, what their fears and dreams were, how easy or difficult their transition had been, and what lessons they had learned along the way.

Hands shot up. I left the meeting with eight names to contact. Word spread. Other women heard about my book and

1

offered to contribute their stories.

Miracle of miracles, my book proposal interested a well-known agent in New York. She spent the better part of a year trying to find a major publisher. "They liked it," she said. "The editors just don't feel the market is big enough. It's a good book, Blue, and one that deserves to be published."

I'm not sure how big the market is, but I decided to publish this book myself so other women might be motivated to change an unsatisfactory life. Getting *Midlife Mavericks* into print has become one of my life's missions.

In the year 2000, an entire generation of baby boomers arrived at midlife. Compared to prior generations, we will live longer, remain healthier, and redefine what it means to be middle-aged. We have survived the conformist fifties, the radical sixties, the feminist seventies, and the ambitious eighties.

Many of us rolled out of the nineties more empowered and self-sufficient than any generation before. Others found themselves alone and barely able to exist on dwindling Social Security stipends.

Moving to Mexico isn't the answer for every woman, but the process we employ in evaluating where we've been and what we want for the remainder of our lives is the same. The underpinning of this book, the common denominator of the stories, is change.

I have divided this book into three sections, each focusing on the various reasons women choose to reinvent their lives in Mexico.

Part I: Is This All There Is?

Careers, corporate ladders, glass ceilings, stock options...heart attacks, ulcers, cancer, and divorce. As young as forty, women are taking a second look at their choices and asking, "Is this all there is?" Burned out, used up, or trapped in unfulfilling careers, an attorney swaps law for painting, a corporate executive gives up prestige to search for purpose, and a manager of a temporary employment agency sheds her trappings for simplicity.

Part II: It Ain't Over Till the Fat Lady Sings

A husband leaves his wife of twenty-nine years; a hospital casts aside a nurse with a silent stroke, penniless; a financial advisor swindles a woman out of her retirement savings late in life. These women pick themselves up, dust themselves off and find their heartaches transformed into blessings as they discover the joy of living solo in Mexico.

Part III: Indiana "Joans"

Born too late to ride westward in covered wagons, these midlife mavericks lust for adventure. They long to experience a new culture, to establish roots in foreign soil, to free themselves of society-imposed roles, and to test their own mettle. These intrepid women hark to the call of the unknown and heed the counsel of Yoda in *Star Wars*: "Try? Try? There is no try. Only do or not do."

As the women between these pages attest, life may begin at forty, but a second or third life can start at age fifty, sixty, or even eighty. I hope our stories, like those of generations of women before us, bring us closer together as we march to a common cadence into the twenty-first century.

During hundreds of conversations with ordinary women who have made extraordinary choices, I have discarded old beliefs and created new dreams. Maybe you will, too. I invite you to grab a cup of coffee, curl up on a cozy couch, and travel vicariously with these marvelous midlife mavericks through the altered landscape of middle age.

Special Notes:
- *The names of the women in these chapters have been changed. Their stories are true.*
- *For currency conversion purposes, 9.3 pesos equaled 1 U.S. dollar at the time of publication.*
- *The terms* gringo *and* gringa *are used extensively*

throughout this book. In Mexico, they are not considered derisive terms, but simply refer to a North American man or woman.

- *These interviews took place over a period of two years. Where I have obtained updated information, I have included that as a postscript at the end of each chapter.*

Part I:

Is This All There Is?

Careers, corporate ladders, glass ceilings, stock options—heart attacks, ulcers, cancer, and divorce. As young as forty, women are taking a second look at their choices and asking, "Is this all there is?" Burned out, used up, or trapped in unfulfilling careers, an attorney swaps law for painting, a corporate executive gives up prestige to search for purpose, and a manager of a temporary employment agency sheds her trappings for a simpler life.

1 | Opting Out

*The trouble with being in the rat race
is that even if you win, you're still a rat.*
Lily Tomlin

"Are you crazy?" Liz asked, her forkful of lemon meringue pie suspended in midair. Her icy green eyes glared at me—first with incredulity, then with accusation. "What will you do, Blue? Where will you live?"

We had cleared the dishes and were retreating to the deck for dessert when I announced to Liz, my best friend of thirty years, "I've sold my house and I'm moving to Mexico."

Liz, in her late fifties, typifies the silent generation, a generation for whom security is a high priority. She has worked for the same company, lived in the same house, and had the same boyfriend for more than a quarter century. Only eight years younger than she, I was born just months before the first baby boomers, epitomizing that group of Americans who value doing, owning, and achieving. Change and challenge were my motivators.

This was one of those rare times the two of us needed to straddle our generation gap. Liz couldn't comprehend my craving for change; and at that moment, I wasn't so sure about it either. Maybe there should be a natural limit to impetuosity—

something like the law of gravity.

When my mother was forty with three kids and in the throes of a difficult divorce, she said more than once, "I've worked hard for a nervous breakdown, I deserve one and, damn it, I'm going to have one." Until now, I hadn't understood her cry for help, yet I hoped Liz and my kids would understand mine. As a marketing consultant, I worked eighty-hour weeks and spent a third of my life on an airplane. Burned out and dead-dog tired, I craved a change of pace.

Liz said, "I need a glass of wine." I served us each one. She took a sip, put the glass down as though she were trying to grind out a cigarette with it, and said with a brisk, military voice, "You've got some talking to do, lady."

I leaned back in my chair, watching the woodpecker store his winter food in one of the fifty-foot-tall redwoods beyond my deck. "Once upon a time," I said, in my best fairy-tale voice. Then I continued my story, as I'll tell it now to you.

A couple months before our barbecue, I'd been in a macho executive meeting where sound business decisions suffered at the hands of politics and power plays. While sitting there in disgust, an invisible force bonked me over the head and whispered, "Run!" It felt like a cold breeze had passed through my body. I shivered.

I shook my head to clear it. Run? Where? Why?

At that instant, I realized I didn't *want* to be there anymore. Furthermore, I didn't *have* to be there anymore. My children were grown and I had never remarried after my on-again, off-again five-year marriage. I was tired of climbing the corporate ladder and knocking my head against the glass ceiling.

Soon after that epiphany, I took a short vacation to visit my mother in Idaho. I needed revitalization. Mom called it "hyacinths for the soul." My last night there, a dream started the wheels of my new life in motion. I woke up repeating the word *enclave* over and over in my mind. Words in dreams are significant, so I got up and found a dictionary. The definition of enclave was "a cultural unit enclosed within a foreign territory." It meant nothing to me and I soon forgot about it.

When I returned home, a complimentary edition of International Living was buried in my stack of mail. My skin prickled as I read the front-page headline: "Lake Chapala—A Retirement Enclave in Mexico." A sidebar described an upcoming "Retire in Mexico" conference in Guadalajara. I read the article three times before making flight and conference reservations.

As the taxi delivered me to the Quinta Real, the last five-star hotel I'd be staying in for a long while, adrenaline raced through my veins. Goose bumps covered my arms. A strange visceral sensation, like a weed, was choking out all reason.

At the reception, I noticed most of the attendees were couples in their sixties and seventies. I asked a hostess if there were any problems for single women living in Mexico. She looked at me wide-eyed and said in her fine Georgian drawl, "Honey, if you're comin' here lookin' for a man, don't. The ones here who aren't already married are gay, ninety, or goin' home on Sunday."

No, I realized, laughing at her wisecrack, I'm not looking for a man. I'm looking for myself.

The next morning I listened with rapture to the speakers' stories. In each of them, I recognized veiled parts of myself. I squirmed in my seat, uncomfortable that these strangers could know so much about me. I wrapped my arms around myself in response to a sudden chill.

In a three-bus convoy the following day, we toured Guadalajara, a majestic old city of 8 million people, complete with Price Club, WalMart, and Sam's. On Sunday, we visited Ajijic, nestled between Mexico's largest lake and the mountains. This quiet cobblestone village seeped into my pores like sunshine on a cold winter day. I closed my eyes and inhaled deeply as a gentle breeze caressed the back of my neck. I wondered if this was how Maria Von Trapp had felt escaping to freedom over her beloved Austrian Alps.

Contrasts assaulted me from every direction. A sombrero'd man, holding a cellular phone to his ear, delivered milk on a donkey. Young Mexican boys with buckets of dirty water washed a Mercedes and a horse, side by side. Vivid magenta and tangerine bougainvillea cascaded over drab cement walls. Only the clamor of automobiles bouncing in and out of potholes interrupted the serenity of the village.

That night, as I dozed off, I imagined myself on a magic carpet, a world away from Silicon Valley—a world away from tension and stress. By morning, my sheets were twisted around my legs. I felt sucked into a vortex of confusion. I was enchanted and, at the same time, apprehensive. It was as if two parts of me were vying for center stage. My usual ways of resolving conflicts and making decisions weren't working, and I wondered if there might be a short circuit in my system.

When I returned home, finances were first on the agenda. My briefcase bulged with data we had received at the conference, including cost-of-living, visa, customs, insurance, economic, and political information. Within a few days, rows and columns peppered my office walls. I chuckled—Ms. Left-Brain Analyst making momentous decisions with a combination of spreadsheets, dreams, and intuition. If it was true, as the conference handouts indicated, that I could live comfortably on $1,000 a month…I closed my eyes, crossed my fingers, and pressed "calculate" on the summary spreadsheet.

Yes! Assuming the stock market didn't crash and California didn't fall into the ocean, I could manage on investments until I was fifty-nine and a half. My home was heavily mortgaged, but there might be enough equity in it to afford an inexpensive adobe dwelling in Mexico.

My dream of working ten fewer years made a quantum leap from wishful thinking to reality. But at what sacrifice? My emotions screamed as though on a roller-coaster ride and my reason rode the merry-go-round, desperately trying to grab the brass ring. I couldn't focus on my job. I missed deadlines. I had headaches. I drank too much. After weeks of agonizing indecision, I turned my quandary over to the universe.

I put my house on the market. If it sold, I would go; if it

didn't, I would stay. Now the decision was out of my hands.

Because of the down market, my real estate agent prepared me for a long sale. But in two weeks she delivered a clean, unconditional offer. I felt like I'd been whacked on the side of my head with the answer. Run.

As the final rays of sun disappeared beyond the horizon, I sat on the deck, hugging my legs and rocking back and forth on the lounge. What was I doing? I feared this was one of the many times when my impulsiveness took hold of the reins and dragged my reason behind the wagon like a broken axle. Licking a salty tear from my lips, I focused on the deep blue spaces among the faint outlines of the towering redwood trees. "God, help me."

"That was two nights ago, Liz." I swirled the wine in my glass, waiting for her reaction. She just shook her head.

"It sounds like you'll *need* God's help with this one, Blue."

I tapped my wine glass against hers. "To friends, to family, and to the future."

Liz reached out and grabbed my hand. The tremor in her voice betrayed her emotion. "Why? You already have it all. You have it right here—family, friends, and career. You can't just leave."

She looked so vulnerable—my little redheaded friend. We'd been part of each other's lives for so long. We had met nearly three decades earlier at a time we were both going through divorces. Our kids think of each other as brothers and sisters. I knew Liz would miss me...perhaps more than my own children, who were in the early stages of their own careers and families.

The night before, I had told my son and daughter I was moving. Tory, a strapping young man of thirty, and his sister, Shoni, a year younger, were both upset with me. They took turns. "Why Mexico?" "It's dirty." "It's dangerous." "It's so far away." "You don't speak Spanish." "There are scorpions and snakes there." "What will you do there?" "Don't you love us anymore?"

It felt like they were slapping me in the face with skepticism and indictments. They were hurt because I hadn't confided in them earlier. Why hadn't I? Perhaps because I didn't want to be talked out of my decision. Perhaps the part of me wanting to run was stronger than the part of me wanting to stay. I had been in this house four years, longer than I'd ever stayed in one place throughout my adult life. They should've known me well enough by now.

"Who will I talk to when I need my mom?" asked Shoni. "And don't tell me we'll have e-mail, it's not the same."

"What can we do to make you stay?" my son asked.

"Grandkids?" I half kidded. Tory and Sandra had been living together for five years and were recently engaged.

"Sandra's just had a three-month contraceptive shot and it takes at least nine months after that."

"Okay, then," I said, trying to muss his short curly hair to no avail, "let's reopen this discussion in another year. Few decisions are final."

My heart hurt. But my kids had their own lives to live and so did I.

Liz ran her finger around the rim of her glass, avoiding my gaze. I softened my voice and placed my hand over hers. "I just know that doing more of what I'm doing and getting more of what I'm getting is not going to make me happy. This can't be all there is."

I walked behind her chair, put my arms around her shoulders, and rested my chin atop her long, curly hair. "We both work so many hours, we don't see each other more than once a month anyway." When I had moved from the Bay Area to the beachside town of Aptos, the extra hour's drive over the dangerous Santa Cruz Mountains had reduced the time we spent together.

"When you visit me in Mexico, we can spend a week or two of quality time together."

"If," she whispered, not responding to my hug.

"And I'll be back to visit."

I walked her to the door and waved goodbye as Liz backed out of the driveway. Maybe she was right. Maybe I was crazy. I'd only been in Ajijic one day. That wasn't enough time to decide I wanted to live there. I had no idea what I would do with my life. I wondered if I could give up my addiction to working. I felt like the blocks had been kicked from in front of the wheels and my wagon was heading out. Would I pick up the reins and lead, or lean back and enjoy the ride?

An old memory nudged its way into my consciousness. With her right foot behind her and her left toes touching a spot three feet ahead, a seminar leader of mine once said, "Most of us live our lives like this, with one foot planted firmly in the past and the other reaching tentatively ahead toward the future. What are we doing? Pissing on the present."

Leaning against the closed door, I took three deep breaths. With each, I pledged my intention to live every moment fully as I ventured into the second half of my life.

2 | In Search of Me

Woman's discontent increases in exact proportion to her development.
Elizabeth Cady Stanton

As the shadows of my avocado tree crept across the lawn, Liz scooped guacamole onto her taco chip and said solemnly, "It's all so different since everything's changed." Her eyes were lowered, but the corners of her mouth curved up just enough to unveil her subtle humor. I leaned back and laughed. "Profound, Liz. Very profound."

She was right, though. Life was as different for me here in Mexico as it remained the same for Liz, whose years marched on in a well-trodden groove, altered naturally by the seasons of time—one more grandchild here, another vacation there.

"I hate it that you're gone. I miss you." This was her first visit since I had left Silicon Valley two years ago. I suspected she'd been punishing me.

Her sea-green eyes danced like Australian opals. I reached across the table to cover her hand with mine. "I'm so glad you're finally here. I'm sorry I've had to schedule interviews during your visit."

"Not to worry. I've brought along some good books." Liz leaned forward, elbows on the table. "Moving to another country would never be an option for me, but it's fascinating to learn why other women would and what makes them stay. Are they all like you? Corporate dropouts?"

"No. Most aren't like me. The women I've talked with have led very different lives and came to Mexico for different reasons. I'm anxious to finish the interviews so I can string together the similarities and differences." I rotated the hanging chair I was sitting in 180 degrees, then back again. Screech. Screech. "I'm learning more about myself through their stories. Perhaps writing this book will be a significant part of my own journey."

Liz stood up, inhaling deeply, "What is that luscious smell? Bougainvillea?"

"No. As gorgeous as the bougainvillea is, it has no fragrance. You're smelling night-blooming jasmine."

Liz turned to face me. "I still don't understand how you could move so far from your friends and family. I'll never understand."

Trying to formulate an answer to her half-question, half-accusation, I reflected on how our friendship had gone the distance. We were unlike in so many ways. I supposed we'd learned to accept our differences and enjoy the many things we had in common—families, friends, travel, crafts, wine, and, above all, half a lifetime of shared memories.

"I can't explain, Liz. I'm searching for me, for the part of me that was buried under all the corporate crap and is crying to get out." She shook her head. She couldn't comprehend. I wished sometimes my life could be as simple as hers—as black and white.

I pushed my foot against the table, swinging the canvas chair to and fro. "Besides, who left whom? Mom moved to Idaho after my step-dad passed away, Shoni moved to Seattle for a better job, and Tory and Sandra are already making plans to leave California."

"*I'm* still there." The twinkle in her eyes tempered a sulky pout.

The screech of metal against metal vied for my attention. My swinging patio chair was welded to a steel beam above the deck, and I was forever checking to make sure it was secure.

"Has it been difficult adjusting to another culture? Starting over?"

"It's always difficult starting over, but I've had lots of practice at that. Normally it takes me about six months to feel comfortable in a new place, to find my way around and develop a new circle of friends. But here, I felt like I belonged by the end of my first week.

"While I was looking at houses, my Realtor schmoozed me, introducing me to other single ladies. Then, at the bed and breakfast I stayed in for a month, I met other folks."

"It's easy for you to meet new people," Liz said. "You're so much more outgoing than I am."

Was I an extrovert or an introvert? That was a hard distinction for me to make about myself. I like people. I laugh a lot. But I also require a lot of time alone. Meeting people here is easy for anyone who's willing to step outside their house. The biggest difficulties for me were not speaking Spanish and feeling out of control. I expected things to work, to be able to fix them myself or at least to know who to call when something went wrong. I'd wait all day for a repairman to show up and work myself into a self-righteous snit because he didn't. Maybe he'd come the next day, maybe the next week. I'd make myself miserable. It didn't bother him, though. If I wasn't home when he came, he'd just try another time. No problem.

"Patience has never been one of your virtues." Liz crunched on a taco chip and checked my reaction out of the corner of her eye.

I chuckled. "Early on I adopted a life rule: If at first you don't succeed, try two more times, then throw the damn thing out the window." I chuckled at a fleeting vision. "I remember the time I adopted that rule. I was a teenager and it was a bad-hair day. I couldn't make my French roll do what I wanted, and after two attempts, I threw the hairbrush into the bathtub. It broke. My hair still looked like crap, but somehow I felt better."

Liz laughed. "I can just picture that. She walked to the

edge of the patio to get a better whiff of the nighttime jasmine.

"I've had to adopt a *qué sera* attitude to keep my sanity in Mexico. I would wait only an hour or two for people to show up, and if they didn't, I just went on about my business. I quickly figured out I couldn't be in charge here. I've been too controlling all my life anyway, so here I get lots of opportunity to practice being out of control. I think it's good for me."

"I guess waiting around matters a lot more when you're working," Liz said. "Now you've got all the time in the world to wait."

"It's funny—and I'm not the only one who says this—but my hours and days fill up. I wonder how I ever managed to fit a real job into my life."

"What do you do, then, to fill up your hours—besides waiting for workers?"

"Everyone asks that question. At first, remodeling my house took all my time. I shopped for thirty-two hours just for living room furniture. Everything takes longer. We pay bills in person, with cash. Sometimes there are long lines. We may have to shop in four stores to complete a grocery list. It may take a week to get a car fixed, and because mechanics don't have phones, it takes several trips to find out whether or not the car is ready.

"After the house was finished and furnished, I took a class on writing fiction and began a novel. I discovered online classes in writing and joined several Internet critique groups. Then I started writing a monthly Internet column, "Living in Mexico: From a Woman's Perspective," and kept busy responding to readers' inquiries.

"I'm making soft-sculptured dolls now. I enjoy going out to restaurants with friends and trekking to nearby cities and villages. We've got a great little theater and lots of cultural events here and in Guadalajara." I thought a minute and added, "Parties, volunteer teaching at the orphanage...and I've had lots of company."

"You're making me tired." Liz shook her head and wandered off to inspect the rest of my garden.

I reflected on how different my choices were from Liz's and those of my mother and grandmother. They had lived during a war. My grandmother grew her own food and Mom worked in canneries to help make ends meet after Dad returned from World War II.

We baby boomers were raised in a land of plenty, quasi-equality, and opportunity. Women were boosted up the career ladder by anti-discrimination legislation and then kicked back down as we reached for the top rung.

"I am woman. I can do anything," Helen Reddy belted out, raising our battle cry. The feminist movement had created turmoil in traditional family relationships. Too many of us who bought into those promises ended up with bulging pocketbooks and sobbing souls. Success often came at the sacrifice of time—time for ourselves and time for our families.

Liz returned to the deck with a bouquet of flowers she'd picked and asked, "So, have you found yourself in Mexico?"

Such a difficult question. I had no idea how to answer her. We sat quietly awhile, listening to the twitter of birds and crickets, lost in our individual thoughts. Liz smiled wistfully and I gazed at the evening clouds, framed by a cobalt sky.

"I think it's time for more wine," I said, dodging her question for the moment. "And you need a vase for those flowers."

I returned to the deck, juggling an orange glass vase and a tray laden with crackers, cheese, and a carafe of wine. Liz had claimed my canvas chair. I filled our glasses. Liz raised hers in a toast. "To best friends. Do you really like it here, Blue? Really?"

"Yes. It's a tropical paradise with few tourists. Life is simple and serene. The weather is perfect. Most gringos here don't work and they have time for new friendships. I've met such interesting people—from all over the world." Liz swayed back and forth in the hanging chair, not saying anything.

"Remember," I said, "when I told you I expected there to be a common denominator of folks here—people who embraced differences, had a high risk tolerance, were full of life, and didn't sit around waiting for death?"

Liz leaned her head against the canvas chair and closed her eyes, trying, I surmised, to understand me. I continued. "No one asks, 'What did you do?' or 'Where did you go to college?' They ask, 'Where do you come from?' 'How did you find out about this place?' and 'Can you join us tonight for dinner?' "

I could tell Liz wasn't on my wavelength, so I tried again. "I have all the time I need now—time for friends, time for family, and time for me. Each day is like a gift. I don't know what it holds for me until I unwrap it. No schedules, no meetings, no employees, no..."

Liz swung around until her back was facing me and asked, "Did you buy the house to prove you were right about moving here or to make sure you stayed?" Zap. Invisible sparks flew at me.

Why had I? I had no intention of buying. My real estate friend offered to show me around the different neighborhoods, just to get the lay of the land. I guess she was smarter than she looked. This house had been deserted for six years and the reigning royalty were ants and termites. It was uninhabitable. New electricity, plumbing, tiles, cupboards, doors, fixtures, and windows would be needed. I purchased it my third day here. It was another impulsive decision.

"I think I needed to decompress. I considered the house a transitional project that would keep me busy, force me to learn the whos and wheres and hows of living in Ajijic, and keep me from hibernating behind closed doors. If I had rented a furnished place, I might have disappeared in front of my computer or into a bottle of wine."

"I'll drink to that," Liz said, swinging around to face me, her glass raised. I smiled at the saying on her T-shirt, "Will Work for Wine," and thought of the hundreds of California art and wine festivals we'd enjoyed over the years.

I reached for the carafe. "It was a scary time for me, Liz. I had to redefine myself as a single woman without a job, without goals or purpose, and without external expectations. I had no support system. I had more questions than answers. Who am I? What is my purpose in life? How do I find fulfillment outside of a career?"

"What do you mean, who are you? You're Blue. You're mother of Shoni and Tory. You're friend of Liz and daughter of Betty. It frustrates me when you talk like this."

"I know." I realized there was no point in continuing this conversation. I stood up, saying, "Let's have a game of ping-pong and then go to dinner. What kind of food do you want? We have Mexican, Chinese, Japanese, German, Lebanese, and American restaurants."

"Winner decides," Liz said, reaching for a paddle "But first, one more question." She walked over to the far end of the ping-pong table. "Why are you always driven to do something different—climb new mountains, move to new countries?"

I bounced the ping-pong ball on the Mexican tile patio while I thought about her question. "I guess that has to do with my father. All my life, my goals were designed to win his approval. 'Look, Dad, I can do it. Are you proud of me yet? Do you love me now?' I realized I was still doing that, even ten years after he died." I threw the ball onto her side of the table to begin the rally. "Not anymore. I'm living the rest of my life to make me happy, not him."

"Atta girl, Blue." Liz slammed the ball back at me. I missed. Her smile was warm and accepting. "And it'll make me happy if you let me win this game."

As we played, I began to think about my next morning's interview with Anna. At age thirty-eight, she had chucked a lucrative legal career and moved to Mexico to challenge herself as an artist. I wondered how similar her story would be to mine.

3 | Reflections on a Canvas

If you always do what interests you, then at least one person is pleased.
Advice to Katherine Hepburn from her mother

I first met Anna at a Tuesday evening salon where local writers and artists gathered to share a potluck dinner and provide feedback on each other's work. This was her first showing at the salon and I was eager to view her art.

Janet, one of the original members of the salon and a friend of Anna's, introduced her to the group. "Anna and I met riding horses on the other side of the lake. She's lived in Jocotepec for two years, rides daily, and, as you can see, is much younger than the rest of us." Janet put her arm around Anna's waist, giving her a playful hug, and Anna blushed. I guessed her age at about forty. Janet continued. "Anna's past life included being a U.S. attorney, but she traded in that life to pursue her art here in Mexico."

Earlier Anna had placed three equal-sized canvases on the floor, facing the wall. "Thank you for inviting me," she said in a soft, reticent voice. "I don't want to influence your reactions, so I'm going to show you my last project without any prior discussion." She turned the first canvas toward us. On it appeared a pair of dark-skinned, high-heeled legs chopped off a few inches above the knee. I squirmed in my seat and sneaked a glance at several of the other members. What?

Next, she balanced the second canvas atop the first. Ah, now the legs disappeared underneath a short black skirt.

Anna asked for a volunteer. Janet supported the two lower canvases while Anna held the third above them. The life-sized black woman on the three canvases wore an African headdress and was depicted with bold, bossy brush strokes. A triptych, Anna called the trio of paintings.

Studying her reactions to the group's feedback, I listened to Anna describe the feelings she had tried to capture with her subject—strength, pride, and vigor.

Shorter than her canvas creation and without makeup, Anna was upstaged. She was earthy—brown hair, brown shirt, and brown eyes. Her quiet, contemplative demeanor provided a sharp contrast to the arrogant African woman in red-and-black garb. Haughty and secure in her beliefs, the painted face exuded determination. I could almost hear her shout: "Say what you will. Do what you must. I will not be oppressed." I imagined Anna had drawn upon a deep reservoir of inner strength to capture this vigorous woman in oil. I wanted to know Anna better. I wondered what she was doing here in the prime of her life.

Following her presentation, I read a chapter from my book, a local potter described her new glazing process, and a poet read a selection from his seafaring collection. After we adjourned, I cornered Anna and asked if she'd grant me an interview.

"I'm a pretty private person," she said. "I'm not sure that would be a good idea."

After I assured her that her story would be anonymous, she reluctantly agreed. "You can't miss my place," she had said, writing down her address and phone number. "It's the two-story orange house crowned with eight-foot-high golden turrets."

Now, as I rounded the corner and caught sight of her house, I smiled. The golden tiles on the turrets refracted the morning sun like a prism, casting a colorful rainbow above her home. Understated and natural, she hadn't struck me as a "turret" type of person.

At the gate, a calf-sized black beast thwarted me. His ears stood at attention. His lips stretched back, exposing incisors that could slice through my wrist with a single bite. He growled. My heart pounded. He smelled my fear. "Nice dog. Nice dog." My voice trembled and I considered getting back into my car.

As Anna opened the gate, her warm eyes welcomed me, and the dog, now docile as a kitten, accompanied us around the side of her home to a small courtyard. Every horizontal surface was strewn with art magazines, literary books, and newspapers. I moved *The Mexico Times* from the nearest chair and sat while Anna fetched some ice water.

"May I have a tour before we begin?" I asked when she returned to the patio.

"Sure. It's a little sparse because most of my furniture is still stateside, but *mi casa es su casa*." I followed her into the house, my five feet seven inches and slightly pear-shaped, carrying a bit of excess weight in her hips.

Paintings, still-life setups, and canvas stretchers were scattered everywhere. A glorious Monet-style woodlands scene, replete with angels, hung prominently above the staircase. A single bed and a lamp were the only pieces of furniture in her living room.

Anna shrugged her shoulders. "At least I don't have anything anyone would want to steal."

Upstairs, a labyrinth of small angled rooms surrounded the stairwell, some with decks, others with more windows and doors than wall space. "Not very practical, some of these rooms," Anna said, "but I love their pluck."

I was amused by her choice of word. I hadn't heard pluck in a long time. "How old is this place?"

"Four years."

Vivid colors garnished the walls, and bright Mexican tiles welcomed guests into the kitchen and bathrooms. Light streamed through the stained-glass insets in the turrets and danced in the living room.

"This house is wonderful, Anna. It's full of personality. Do you own it?"

She shook her head. "I'm renting. It's 2,500 square feet and really more than I need, but it was a steal at $450 a month."

I'd had no idea there was anything this nice in Jocotepec. "Let me know if you ever move. I'd love to live here."

"I'll put your name on the list." Her smile was reserved. "I don't like living in the Americanized communities. Here, I've the convenience of modern plumbing and electricity, great light for my painting, and the joy of being within walking distance of the plaza. Best of all, I rarely see any gringos."

I grabbed at my stomach, grimacing in mock pain.

"Present company excepted." Anna redeemed herself with another, less reserved, smile. The few gringos living in Jocotepec have assimilated into the community, so Jocotepec, the town, has retained its authentic Mexican look and feel—unlike Ajijic, with its many North Americans, international restaurants, and cultural events.

I wondered how difficult it would be to get along in a village like this with my limited grasp of the language. "Are you fluent in Spanish?" I asked.

"I am now. My French and Italian helped me learn quickly."

"I envy you because I struggle with the language. I've taken two months of intensive Spanish lessons in Guadalajara—five hours a day, five days a week. But living in Ajijic, where most everyone speaks English, I get precious little opportunity to practice it. Even if I order in Spanish, the waiter responds in English. Sometimes that irritates me."

"They want to practice their English, too." Anna cocked her head and raised her eyebrows with a "Sorry, but them's the breaks" kind of look.

We settled into painted rattan chairs among the myriad of potted plants that adorned her courtyard. I asked her to tell me about her life pre-Mexico.

She zigzagged me across the years and continents of her life without mentioning her career in law.

Remembering how much I had been defined by my job in various careers, her omission surprised me. Was it a total lack of ego, or had she really disassociated herself from the legal profession, from her professional identity?

"How did you discover Jocotepec? It's not exactly on the tourist trail."

She corrected my pronunciation. "Accent on the first and last syllables. It's an Indian name. **Ho**.ko.tay.**peck**."

Anna stretched her Levi legs in front of her and began. "The Belgian job I took after Mom died required extensive travel to Guadalajara. I also spent a lot of time in Peru at a ceramics factory. I considered that a temporary situation, because my dream was to buy a farm in Vermont, get a horse, and begin painting again. But then I started feeling very comfortable in Mexico. I tried to negotiate a permanent transfer with my employer; but I was unsuccessful, so I resigned and moved here on my own.

"One weekend while I was living in a hotel in Guadalajara, I saw an ad for a gallery exhibit by Georg Rauch in Jocotepec. He's a seventy-one-year-old artist whose work I have admired for a long time. We began talking art and he invited me to visit again. I really liked it here and I'd had my fill of big-city life. Jorge turned me on to this house, and here I am." Anna extended her hands, palm side up. *"Fâit accompli."*

"I understand you were once an attorney. Why did you decide to give that up?"

Anna chewed on the inside of her lower lip. "I was comfortable as an attorney and good at it. Then, very slowly, this sense of dissatisfaction began to ooze over me. I felt like what I was doing wasn't making a tremendous difference, and eventually I realized I was becoming unhappy."

Her story reminded me of that moment I had decided to chuck corporate America. I wondered if men had such epiphanies; and if so, did they act on them?

"If I had stayed longer," she continued, "I'd have done

what everyone else did and become trapped like they were."

I raised my eyebrows in question and she explained. "I'd invest in real estate I couldn't afford, knowing my salary would continue to increase. Then I'd be locked into a mortgage and all dreams of freedom would die. I knew this was the last time I could still make a choice."

I nodded. "Before you became a slave to your possessions." I understood exactly what she meant.

Her dog barked ferociously at a passerby and Anna called to him. "Quiet, Gar." Once he had returned to her side, she began again. "Finally, I reached a point where I couldn't sleep for several nights. That was unusual for me. I knew something was wrong and it was up to me to correct it. During those fretful nights, I dreamed I was painting again. I felt joyful. It had been a long time.

"I realized I wanted very much to pursue my art. There was no way for me to squeeze that time into my hundred-hour weeks, so I asked for a leave of absence from the firm."

"Did you get it?"

"Yes, although none of us believed I'd come back."

I imagined that Anna, like me, had spent little time looking back. "When you left, did you discover that a lot of your self-identity, your self-esteem, was wrapped up in your job?"

Anna stretched her legs, crossing them at the ankles, put her hands behind her head, and gazed at something beyond me. "No, not really. Maybe I hadn't been there long enough, but after I stopped practicing law, a strange thing happened. At cocktail parties, people would invariably ask what I did. When I could no longer say I was an attorney at such-and-such law firm, I became socially invisible. Hmm, I haven't thought about that in a long time."

"I know exactly how you felt. When I left Hewlett-Packard after sixteen years to start my first company, I ended up telling people I was self-unemployed." Anna chuckled. "It was easier than trying to explain who I was or what I did. I had no clients, no contracts, and hadn't completed my business plan. If I couldn't define myself, how could I expect others to?

It was a difficult time."

"This life is so much easier, so much more fulfilling. I'm learning who I am a little more each day...and it's not Anna Parker, attorney-at-law."

I tried to picture Anna in a three-piece navy-blue suit with briefcase at her side. It was difficult. Of course, who was I to talk? Pantyhose hadn't touched my legs since I left Silicon Valley.

"There are some parallels in our lives, Anna. It was a dream, too, that brought me to Ajijic. And that was out of character for me. During my career, I had made most of my decisions with spreadsheets and decision trees."

She smiled.

"Maybe," I said, "we're a couple of gals who developed our left brains first and then, when they got too big for our heads, we escaped in order to work on our right brains."

Deep in thought, Anna nodded. "Let's talk more about that another time. Right now, I'm going to refill our glasses, and then I'd like to hear about the dream that brought you to Mexico."

4 | **Mirror! Mirror!**

It's better to have a rich soul than to be rich.
Olga Korbut

Asking about my dream was, I supposed, Anna's way of procrastinating.

There was no hurry and I hoped to have a new friend in Anna. Perhaps if I exposed some of my own vulnerability, she'd open up. Building friendships, I knew, was about trust, caring, and common experiences. Listening to other women's stories often enables us to strengthen a resolve to fulfill our own dreams.

I took a sip of water, leaned back in my chair, and began to talk about my dreams.

"I've always been an incessant dreamer—Technicolor, sound, three-act scenes, multiple dreams. Right before I moved to Mexico, I began to study dreams as a way of getting in touch with my deeper self. Even my left-brain realized the symbols and words in dreams must come from inside me. I figured if I could tap into that inner knowledge, my life might be more rewarding."

Anna's gaze remained steady. She seemed to be devouring every word. "After I had attended the Retire in Mexico conference in Guadalajara and visited Ajijic, I went home very confused. I felt like I was on a teeter-totter, and an old Jimmy Durante song, "Have you ever had the feeling that you wanted to go, but you wanted to stay, but you wanted to go?" played persistently in my head.

"Different parts of me vied for control, struggling to be recognized by the podium. 'Go.' 'Stay.' 'You can't run away from yourself.' 'Run.' 'What are you running toward?' Anna, can you understand?"

She nodded. "Like me trying to choose between becoming an artist and being an attorney. Freedom or fame? Security or sensitivity?"

"Yes, exactly like that. Tell me more about your inner struggle. How did you handle it? Do you feel you've reached a resolution?"

"*After* your dream." Anna shook her forefinger at me as though I'd been caught taking a bite out of a See's chocolate and putting it back in the box in favor of another.

"Okay." I understood this was a very subtle power play, and with some patience, it could become a win-win.

I was in a large office building. My co-workers were admonishing me for being so impulsive and pleading with me not to leave (they knew I was moving to Mexico). I didn't want to hear any more, so I left the building, drove off, and somehow made a wrong turn. The road became increasingly narrow and steep until I couldn't drive any further. I got out of the car, kicked it hard, and stomped off. The path disappeared and I found myself up to my knees in mud, unable to move forward or back. Exhausted from my struggle, I finally gave up.

"I'm no expert, Blue, but that definitely sounds like you were stuck somewhere in your life." I gave Anna thumbs up and continued.

At that exact moment of surrender, a sparkling clear river meandered by. I dove in. The water embraced me like a womb and I experienced an emptiness of mind and a freedom of spirit I'd never known before.

The river placed me gently upon an expanse of maize-colored plains. Many miles beyond stood a range of muted mauve mountains. The scene reminded me of a canvas with only the background painted, waiting to come alive under an artist's brush.

"Sometimes dream scenes are the basis for my own paintings," Anna said. "Maybe you're a repressed painter yourself."

"Not me. I can't draw or carry a tune. Or whistle, or spit watermelon seeds." I glanced at Anna to see her reaction. "My friend once called me 'orally disabled,' but I can tie a cherry stem into a knot inside my mouth."

Anna laughed, then perched one foot on the edge of her chair and rested her chin on a knee. "I can see how clearly that dream pointed you away from your old life and toward a new land." She hugged her leg. "Sometimes it's just paying attention to the signs, isn't it?"

I nodded.

"Have you filled in the rest of the canvas yet?" Her eyes twinkled. She'd just grabbed the baton again. I shook my head. Anna's spirituality and essence were seeping into her conversation. This was good...very good. I had glimpsed this side of her at our salon, but she was an expert at hiding behind her words and protecting her privacy.

"Now, Ms. Parker," I commanded, "back to your story."

"Okay, okay, okay." Anna stretched out her arms and legs and talked more about where she'd lived and what she'd done—nonthreatening subjects.

"When I lived in Belgium, I designed tile murals. It was a way to paint without having my fragile ego on the line, but my heart wasn't in it. I realize now that job served its purpose by baby-stepping me to a new life in Mexico."

"As an ex-attorney, did you make a list—either mental or on paper—of the pros and cons of living in Mexico?"

"Hunh unh. I felt comfortable in Mexico. I'm good with

languages and it's always been easy to integrate myself into foreign communities. In fact, I believed it would be less stressful settling in Mexico than returning to the East Coast after having lived overseas."

Perhaps only an expatriate would understand that conclusion. I had experienced reverse culture shock when my kids and I returned from Germany in the early eighties. You're prepared for everything to be different when you move to another country, but you expect things to be the same when you return. They never are. Your peers have moved up the ladder and you've changed in subtle ways that may take years to understand.

Anna continued with her pros and cons. "The cost of living was less here, which meant my savings would last longer. On the other hand, the likelihood of meeting a mate was not as good in Mexico as in the States." Anna looked up and pursed her lips, trying to remember. "I had no concerns about safety. Really, there were no terrific downsides. I could always go back."

"Have you been married?"

She picked a small leaf off the table and studied it. "No. No marriage. No children."

"Is that important to you? You're still young enough to have a family."

Still examining the leaf, she said, "I'm a very independent person. Perhaps if I were born a generation later, there would be more men to choose from who respected that in a partner; but I've met precious few who could fit into my life without taking away my alone time for riding, reading, and painting. In this society where Mexican men are macho and traditional in their beliefs about women's roles, I think it would be next to impossible to find the right man." Anna poked the ice cubes under the water in her glass, watching them bob up and down. "Perhaps marriage and family isn't ordained for me in this life. I'm doing a great deal of work on myself, and other responsibilities might get in the way."

The audible period at the end of her last sentence indicated it was time to change the subject.

"And has it worked out well for you here? Are you happy in Mexico?"

"Yes. All my neighbors and most of my friends are Mexican—sometimes I can even pass for Mexican. I love it when that happens." Her skin color was light olive.

Anna leaned back with a big smile. "One of my highlights was being invited to participate as a bridesmaid in my neighbors' son's wedding. These people are like family to me. They have five grown children, ages nineteen to thirty, and twin grandchildren. We eat together four or five times a week."

"It sounds like you've fully integrated into Jocotepec. Think you'll stay here?" I remembered her comment about not shipping her furniture here until she was sure what she wanted to do.

"Hmm. If more expatriates settle here, I'll probably move further away. But I love Mexico. I'll be here for a long time. Of course, my painting will have to start supporting me or I'll be forced to get another job." Anna scowled.

"Remember when career meant everything?" I asked. It wasn't long ago for either of us, yet it seemed a lifetime away.

Anna reached down to pet Gar and looked up at the sky. "You know, even though I came from a highly paid, egocentric career, I'm much prouder of being here than I ever was of being an attorney."

"No regrets?"

"No, but I am aware I may have sacrificed something really safe for my art, which is much riskier. I hope I haven't miscalculated."

"What if you have?"

"I'd have to go home and find something else to do. That's the worst case. But it's much better to figure out what you love doing and do it as best you can; otherwise, you'd probably always wonder what would have happened, what your life would have been like if you had reached for your dream and succeeded."

She leaned back in her chair and finished off her water. "I

think if you really want something, the gods are kind. Things work out."

The word *work* triggered another question I had wondered about. "Tell me, since you've worked in several countries, what do you see as the major differences?"

"Obviously, it varies in each culture. Contrary to popular belief, Mexicans are very talented and hardworking. The major challenge here is that the bedrock beliefs and values are different. And their notion of time and commitment creates problems when working across cultures."

"Can you be more specific?"

"Most of us make jokes about *mañana* and chock it up to the Mexicans' disdain for time, but many times, things don't happen on time because more things go wrong here than in the States or Western Europe. Working in Tlaquepaque in the rainy season when metal goods need to be lacquered or varnished can cause delays. The humidity is too high and drying time could slow down production for up to a week.

"Sometimes there will be terrible flooding and the power will go out; other times the workers have a religious fiesta, are hung over and unable to work the next day."

I chuckled. Fiestas were usually on Sundays, and Monday mornings weren't the best time to make appointments.

"Then there's the problem with communication. Mexicans tell you what you want to hear. It's difficult to work under these circumstances. I've learned to phrase my questions differently. If I ask a leading question, such as 'Did you see a young man with a red sweater go by on a green bicycle?' Everyone will say yes because they don't want to disappoint me."

I thought back to the time two American girlfriends and I got lost near Delores Hidalgo because we followed directions that the locals gave us. They always tell you where something is, even if they don't know, because making you happy *now* is more important than having you disappointed or lost *later.* Fortunately, the drug squad rescued us. By that time, we'd run out of gas and were on a road that wasn't even on our map. One man siphoned gas from his own truck and poured it into my tank.

I asked him what the insignia on the back of his black shirt meant and he said, *"Drogas."* When I looked confused, he explained. *"Marijuana, opio, cocaina."* Then I understood, and with my limited Spanish replied, "No, thank you. I prefer tequila." We had a good laugh and they directed us to San Miguel de Allende. They wouldn't take a peso for the gas and they didn't search my Mazda for drugs. I guess three middle-aged American women lost and out of gas in a sexy red MX weren't too suspect.

When we waved goodbye to the armed guards, my friend said, "I was so frightened when I saw those men and their guns."

It had never occurred to me to be frightened. As soon as I saw them, I thought, Angels. Angels have been brought to save us. Knowing how kind and helpful the Mexicans are when someone is in trouble paints a different reality than reading U.S. papers filled with warnings and stories of crime in Mexico.

Returning from my muse, I asked Anna, "Did you find it difficult being a single American woman working with Mexican men?"

"No, not really. The big issue is language, and since I could communicate with them in Spanish and because I knew how to listen past the obvious answers, I had very few problems. That being said, an American or Canadian who is not integrated into the Mexican culture would have a very different experience."

Anna sucked on an ice cube before speaking. "I'd also caution people who think it's easy to do business in Mexico that they must work very hard to make enough money. It's not a good place to come with a dream in one pocket and a thousand dollars in the other. I live modestly in order to give myself as much time as possible. I have a two-year cushion left from my investments and I hope that's enough time to prove my worth as an artist."

"I'm not an artist, Anna, or even a well-versed student, but your work shows a lot of passion, a lot of energy. Are you happy with the direction your painting has taken since moving here?"

Anna wriggled in her chair before answering. "Yes. Yes, I am. It's like a mirror to my soul. I'm learning to slow down and not run away from problems in my life. I feel very strong and free here. The more I know about me, the more my art improves. My work is becoming much freer and more emotionally explicit."

She lowered her voice and continued. "Sometimes I wonder what my life would be like if I lived somewhere else with a different mix of people, but it's kind of an idle concern."

"Do you get bored or feel lonely?"

"Sometimes, sure. But that's true wherever I live. I think boredom has more to do with me than with Mexico. On the other hand, when I have too many things planned for the week, I want to cancel everything. I'm suddenly sick. I'm allergic to people." She shivered. "I don't use a calendar here—I don't want to have my life planned, I just want it to unfold in front of me."

It was my turn to shiver. I was interviewing a woman I'd met only once before and yet she was so like me. She followed dreams and used many of the same expressions I use. In the same way her art was a reflection of Anna, she held up a mirror for me. Both of us had given up successful, prosperous careers; Anna for painting, me for...I still didn't know. I envied Anna her clear path, her certain conviction, her talent for painting.

Anna sat up straight in her chair, folding her hands in front of her. "I'm going to show my work at a gallery in Puerto Vallarta this year. It's scary, but I need to know whether I'm good enough."

"You're good enough. I'm sure of it." I reached across the table to squeeze her hand.

"It's funny." Anna placed her other hand on top of mine. "I came here for reasons I've already mentioned, but I stay because I'm learning new lessons from the Mexicans—lessons on how to live."

"Like what?"

"They have unlimited tolerance. They're much less materialistic people than we are and infinitely more spiritual. Their generosity and caring are wonderful attributes. And the people have time—time to talk and time to listen."

Anna was right. These were lessons we were both learning. In the States, even if our paths had crossed, we wouldn't have taken the time to get to know each other. Here we have all the time in the world, and as we discard the many masks we've accumulated, we see that we are more alike than we are different.

Perhaps, I thought, underneath the layers of oil, Anna and her painted African woman were also kindred spirits.

When I returned home, Liz was on the patio reading a book. "How was it?" she asked.

"Really nice. I very much liked this woman. She was a bit guarded at first, but I think she has a gentle soul, a wise old soul, inside her. We had some great *birria* on the plaza. It's usually a goat stew but is sometimes made with beef. They cook it in huge cauldrons right next to the table. That, plus some tortillas and a cold beer—yummy."

"Will you take me one day?"

"Sure, let's go Thursday. It's market day. In fact, we can go to the spa at San Juan Cosala on the way back. They have many pools of different temperatures from natural springs. It's quite nice.

"I've got two more interviews scheduled and then I'm through for this week. One is tomorrow morning. I'll drop you off at the Ajijic market for a couple of hours, then meet you at Salvador's for lunch."

"Okay, but I have a request. Would you mind if I read some of your interviews? I find this process fascinating."

"Why not?" I retrieved two completed chapters from my office and handed them to her. "Here you go, *amiga*. One is about a Canadian woman who travels around the world by herself, and the other is about a woman who was dumped by her husband after twenty-nine years of marriage. Enjoy."

Postscript:

Twelve months after the interview, Anna met and married a Mexican man, Armando, who has two sons, seven and nine. They live on the other side of the lake raising exotic birds and horses. Armando is a former attorney. I recently attended a baby shower for Anna, who is eight months pregnant with her first child at age 42. She looks great and exudes happiness. It's a boy!

5 | **Sweet Simplicity**

It is best to learn as we go, not go as we have learned.
Leslie Jeanne Sahler

I drove Liz to the *tianguis*, parked the car, and pointed down the street. "I'll meet you at Salvador's for brunch in about an hour. It's the orange building on the corner."

"Take your time," Liz replied. "If I finish with the market early, I'll wander through the stores. You know how I like to shop."

I handed her the car keys. "In case you buy big stuff." Then I walked three blocks to Angie's house. As I approached her gate, she opened it, allowing a tall man with a tiny Chihuahua under his arm to pass through. When he left, we started down the path toward her front door and the bell rang. Re-opening the gate, Angie admitted her friend Roger. After introductions, he asked her, "Was that the exterminator who just left?"

She put her hands on her hips and looked confused. "No, he was a friend from the other side of the lake. His home was flooded last night and he was looking for a dry place to perch."

"Oh," Roger said, looking at his shoes and trying to hide his grin. "I thought with that rat underneath his arm, he might be the exterminator." We all had a good laugh. Roger handed a file folder to Angie and said, "I need you to type this up for me, please. I'll stop by this evening to pick it up." She nodded.

"How did you two fare last night in the downpour?" I asked.

"Wasn't it wonderful?" Angie hugged herself. "I got up in the middle of the night to watch the thunder and lightning show. I don't think I've seen it rain that hard in ten years."

"You should have seen it downtown," Roger said, "Avenida Colon was a raging river. I would have been swept away if I'd tried to cross the street. No wonder they have eighteen-inch curbs."

"Ah, but everything smells so clean this morning," I said, taking in a deep breath. "I only wish I'd left my car out last night. It needs a good bath."

Angie led us inside, and while the two of them finished up business, I scanned her house. A purple concrete fireplace dominated the small living room, complemented by soft lavender walls. Floor-to-ceiling white wood bookcases covered the east end, overflowing with books. In the dining room, a jigsaw puzzle of tropical birds remained partially completed atop a glass table, and tucked into one corner of the dining room, a small computer desk held a scattering of bills and reference books.

Dressed casually in black leggings and a long white T-shirt, Angie had not bothered to put on makeup. Even barefaced, she would turn heads. Her striking silver-white hair waved across her forehead and faded into short dark-gray hair at the sides and nape of her neck. Her small home reflected simple, rustic tastes. Off the living room/dining room, I could see a Mexican tiled kitchen and one bedroom. Clay masks and colorful Mexican tapestries hung on the walls, providing a rich fiesta for the eyes.

Roger left and Angie held up half a bottle of Coke. "Would you like one?"

I shuddered at the thought of coke at nine a.m. and wondered if she also ate cold pizza for breakfast. I shook my head. "Is it possible to have coffee?"

"Only possible. I know I have instant, but…" She went into the kitchen, rummaging through the cupboards. "Success! I think there's just enough for one brewed cup, but you'll have to make it. I don't do coffee."

I poured the grounds into a glass carafe and added boiling water. While it steeped, we sat at the puzzle table and began the interview. "What was your life like before Mexico?"

Angie crossed her legs and, in a soft but authoritative voice, said, "Until 1987, I ran a temporary personnel agency like Kelly Girls. That was right around my fortieth birthday. I'm fifty-three now." She made a temple out of her long, thin fingers. "You know how fate works sometimes?" I nodded, chuckling to myself. Inevitably, fate, serendipity, and synchronicity crept into these interviews.

"I was bored with my job and looking at forty more years of the same. I'd been in Personnel all my life. I wanted to see the world. I wanted to travel. I had a longtime girlfriend, Tamara, who had lived in the same condo complex I did. Years ago, after a divorce, she had moved to Mexico with her two young sons. They lived in San Miguel de Allende. Tamara continuously raved about her experiences there. She used words like 'exotic' and 'amazing.' She continually encouraged me to try something different in my life."

Looking up, Angie slowly twisted an etched silver ring around her finger. "About that same time, at a friend's wedding, I met a man who blathered on about how great Mexico was. Signs pointing toward Mexico seemed to be coming out of the woodwork."

Her eyes mesmerized me. Angie's transparent sea-foam-green irises seemed to float underneath her lids. She drummed her fingernails on the table in a repetitive motion. "You know what it's like when you're finally ready to listen to something you might not have heard previously?"

"Mm hmm. When the student is ready, the teacher appears?"

"Exactly. Shortly after my friend's wedding, Jim, another longtime friend of mine, offered me the opportunity to come to Mexico for the summer and chaperone his 21-year-old daughter. My fortieth birthday loomed on the horizon. I had no responsibilities or financial obligations, so I figured, Why not? I quit my job, rented out my condo, and headed south with Jim and Marcy."

"You had enough saved at the age of forty to live for the next forty years on a human relations salary?"

"I'd had only three jobs—all with great retirement plans and stock option programs. I'd invested to the max in these programs and had been successful with my stock portfolio. I also had that condominium in Sarasota, which I could rent for more than my mortgage payment. My finances were straight. I had no credit problems, and it seemed like a great time to leave. Jim was offering me lodging for the summer at no cost."

"Children?"

"I was married once for seven years, but no children. Really, I had no responsibilities to anyone but myself."

A little green monster perched on my shoulder. I wished that I could have retired at forty instead of fifty-one, but then I'd raised two children on my own. Having them in my life more than compensated for the additional ten years of work. "Why didn't Jim chaperone his own daughter?"

"As a silver merchant, he traveled back and forth to the States for three- to four-week periods. He didn't want to leave Marcy here by herself. His mission was to give his daughter a summer in Mexico—the last vacation before she left home. We celebrated her twenty-first birthday and my fortieth in Mexico."

"That was thirteen years ago?" Angie nodded. "Do you remember your first impressions of Mexico, your fears and delights?"

"I'll never forget that first day. We left the Camino Real Hotel in Guadalajara, via taxi, to check out rentals at the Lakeside. Jim had been here before and liked the area." Angie leaned forward, straining the muscles in her thin neck. "The road between here and Guadalajara was not the four-lane divided highway it is today. All the little pueblos on the side of the road reeked of poverty. I remember asking myself, Am I going to have to live here? Then we went to the supermarket, and seeing all those carcasses hanging on the racks covered with flies, I asked myself again, Am I going to have to shop here? It was awful.

"Were you ready to go home?"

"No. I knew I could handle anything. I had grown up spending every summer of my life on a farm with neither running water nor indoor plumbing. I had a lot of experience roughing it. I just wondered why anybody would choose to do so. I knew I'd have to make adjustments." She stared at the puzzle. "I soon discovered that pleasant adjustments, like having a maid and never washing a dish or ironing a blouse again, offset the inconvenient adjustments like spending an entire day going from store to store to find what you needed for the house."

"Did the maid cook for you, too?"

"No. Marcy and I had enough money that we went out to eat each night. We loved exploring every restaurant and discovering new foods." She laughed. "The first time I cooked, I didn't realize the oven temperature was measured in Celsius rather than Fahrenheit, and I burned our meal."

Angie reached over and fitted in a puzzle piece, saying, "Ta-da!" Then she leaned back in her chair and continued. "I quickly adapted to life in Mexico—to the wonderful climate, to the altitude. I'd only lived at sea level before, and I enjoyed lying on the *mirador* [roof patio] and gawking at the beautiful mountains.

"We had very few phones then. People got together in the evening to play board games. We met at a place called Big Mama's El Tepanco. It means the attic. If you didn't show up for a few nights, someone would come to your house and make sure you were okay, because they couldn't pick up the phone and call. People cared about each other. I felt like I belonged to an extended family."

Angie leaned her head back and swallowed the last of her Coke. "I have great memories of going to the Old Posada,

which is a restaurant and bar right on the lakefront, to open my
mail each day. Because of the high cost of international telephone calls, mail was a big deal." Her coy smile suggested she
was reliving a private memory. "No matter what time of day or
night you went to the Old Posada, someone you knew would
invite you to sit at their table."

"Did you know Spanish when you came?"

"I'd taken Spanish in high school and college and worked
with a lot of Cubans in Miami. Getting to know the Mexicans
and improving my Spanish were priorities for me. I wanted to
know about their culture, their fiestas. They accepted me very
quickly. I also got to know some of the families at the School
for the Deaf, where I volunteered. And the woman who runs
the family planning clinic in Jocotepec introduced me to her
staff of young professional women."

Angie pointed to the pot of coffee sitting behind me on
the table. "You going to drink that or not?"

I plunged the filter down through the brown liquid, com-
pressing the muddy sediment at the bottom, and poured myself
a cup. "After your summer with Jim and Marcy, you just
stayed?"

"Oh yes. The climate, the cost of living, and the small-
town feeling suited me. I went home to Sarasota, had a garage
sale, found a tenant for my condo, and drove back down."

"Were you on a tourist visa?"

"Yes. Every six months I had to return to the States and
renew it. Either I drove 720 miles to the nearest border or I
flew back on vacation to Chicago or Florida. Now, with my
FM3 resident visa, I can renew it annually right here at the
Lakeside." Angie's bare feet rocked on the floor, heel to toe,
heel to toe.

"Have you lived in this house since you moved here?"

"No—only for five years. For the first three and a half
years, I was fortunate enough to housesit for friends. I didn't
receive any remuneration, but I also had no housing costs. I
stopped doing that when a friend's cat was near death by the
time they returned from a trip. I probably felt worse than if it

had been my own pet. After that, I just couldn't do it anymore. This house is just big enough for me—like my condo in Sarasota. It has one bedroom and requires very little maintenance. I can just lock the doors, take off, and not worry about it."

I looked through the dining room window at her front courtyard. Bougainvillea vines climbed up the front wall. A magnificent tree dominated her brick patio, which was lined with a few potted plants. "What kind of tree is that?"

"Avocado." I looked closer. Maybe thirty baby avocados lay on the brick floor. She followed my gaze. "The storm last night. It's Mother Nature's way of pruning."

"Do you do a lot of traveling within Mexico?" I asked.

"I did until I started working. That tied me down a lot."

"Let's talk about your job. I think that's where I met you—in the bookstore. Did you open up the store?"

"Yes. I stocked and arranged the books, but it wasn't my business. The Portalibros is an English-language consignment bookstore. It was an outcropping of Barbara's Bazaar, which sold used furniture and junk on consignment. The books outgrew the room containing them, so the owner and I decided it might be nice to open a separate bookstore." Angie chuckled. "Be careful what you ask for." I raised my eyebrows in question, and she answered. "I went in often to buy books. I'd marvel at the diversity of his selection. I also criticized the lack of organization. He said, 'Maybe you'd like to fix this?' I accepted the gauntlet and the rest, as they say, is history."

"Did you need working papers?"

"Yes. The owner applied for them and justified getting my working permit because of my degree in English literature. I needed official translations of my college diploma and a current FM3."

"You worked full time?"

"From nine to five, six days a week."

"Why? Because you needed the extra money or you were getting bored?" To me, working forty-eight hours a week didn't sound like a very appealing thing to do when you were retired.

Angie laughed and tossed her head back. "No, I didn't

need the job and I wasn't bored. My interest was piqued. I had an opportunity to get my hands on all those books and to be part of a fledgling business. The community received it very well. I even began selling books on the Internet. Our inventory included excellent hardbacks on seafaring, treasure hunting, and exploring. Some were real antiques."

I looked directly into Angie's eyes. "You're young, relatively speaking, and single. How's your romantic and dating life been here?"

"I've had wonderful experiences meeting people who don't live here, but have traveled through the area. I've dated many professional men from Guadalajara and Mexico City."

"Are you talking about Mexican men?"

"Yes. I'm not interested much in the expat community, because most of the men are married. Single men don't seem to move here. If they do, they're either gay, waiting to die, or retarded military." She chuckled and went into the kitchen for another Coke.

"I think it's easier for women to adjust to this life than it is for men," Angie said as she returned to the table, rubbing the top of an open Coke bottle with the bottom of her shirt. "Men often become dissatisfied or bored because they have no hobbies outside of their job. Women tend to multitask and have more outside interests. There's no reason to be bored here. Whatever your interest, you can always find a group of like-minded individuals—from the American Legion to the garden club to the bridge club."

"Any advice to women who might consider moving here?"

Angie lowered her bottle to the table. "It's become much easier to live in Mexico than it was when I moved here. We have telephones and the Internet. The average age of retirees is lower because of the baby boomers." She scooted down and rested her elbows on the arms of her chair. "When I first arrived, it reminded me of Venice, Florida, a retirement community." She reflected another few seconds and then added, "If a woman is used to being single in the States or Canada, she should be comfortable here. Her social life might slow down a bit. On the other hand," Angie raised her Coke bottle as though offering a toast, "it might accelerate, because she'll be the new face in town."

"What about safety?" I asked.

"Here in the village, I don't worry about safety. This is a very populated area. The taco stand on the corner is open late into the night, and they would see if I was in any danger coming or going. When I lived behind the Danza del Sol hotel, I had to get out of the car, open a large gate, and drive down a long driveway. I can remember feeling nervous because it was so dark and isolated. But nothing ever happened."

"Are you one of the brave ones who drive in Guadalajara?" I asked.

"Yes, after so many years, I know my way around. It seems like I drive in every week, either for a doctor's appointment, a movie, dinner, or some errand that can't be accomplished here."

"You mentioned doctors' appointments. What do you do for medical insurance?"

"I have IMSS, the Mexican social insurance, but I've never used it. I keep it in case of major medical problems. For seven years, I carried U.S. health insurance, paying those outrageous premiums every month. Finally I decided if I was going to live here, I'd get Mexican insurance. For regular doctors' visits I just go to a doctor and pay his fee. It costs between $15 and $30 U.S. dollars, depending on the specialty. I also have Mexican plates and a Mexican driver's license."

"And now you work no more."

"I left the bookstore eight months ago."

"That must have made a dramatic change in your life."

"Sure. I'd been working forty-eight hours a week and then I'd spend Sunday at the flea market in Guadalajara, looking for more books."

"Where?"

"The big *baratilla*. It rambles on for about thirty blocks and includes a combination of new stuff and old stuff. Lots of old furniture and old books. La Baratilla—it means 'the little cheap.' "

"And what's your life like now, after your second retirement?"

"Nice. I recently spent ten days touring the Yucatan. Next month, I'm heading to the States for sixty days to spend the Fourth of July in Chicago, visit my family and friends, and meet my new tenant in Florida. I've read many of the books I had piled up in the corner. My life is simpler. It's easier to keep the household running when you don't have to go to work every day. I do volunteer work for the School for the Deaf at fundraisers. It's hard to tell at the end of the day what I've accomplished, but I've normally got some project going."

She chuckled. "I can always find a way to spend money going out to lunch or dinner and find someone to do it with. I don't do a lot of grocery shopping because I live alone and eat simply."

I watched for changes in Angie's facial expression as I asked, "What does it cost you to live here?"

She didn't flinch. "I keep track of everything I spend. It costs me between $800 and $1200 a month, depending on whether or not I've incurred a big expense in any one month. I don't prorate those expenses. My rent is $250, not including utilities or my maid."

I leaned forward. "Was there ever a time you regretted your move here?"

"Never. And my decision is reinforced every time I go home to visit. I can't believe my friends are still involved in the rat race and all that consumerism. They say, 'Oh, I envy you so much.' " Angie shook her head slowly back and forth smiling like a Cheshire cat. "I keep telling them, 'Follow me. I can show you the way.' "

After a brief goodbye hug, I walked back to meet Liz at Salvador's, glad I'd had the opportunity to meet Angie.

Liz waved from a table near the rear window. She'd downed half a cup of coffee and had waited for me before ordering. "Try the *huevos Mexicanos*, I suggested. They're scrambled eggs with onions and salsa. Not too hot."

We ordered, and as the waiter left to get my coffee, Liz asked, "Well?"

"Hmm. A very interesting woman."

"Interesting. I hate that word. It doesn't tell me anything. And you, a writer. Pick some more descriptive words." I laughed. "Angie has a quiet strength about her. She's learned to go with life's ebbs and flows and reach out for opportunity when it floats by. "She retired at forty. I guess with no kids to support, you can really sock away the money. How was the tianguis?"

"I loved it. The fruits and vegetables are so beautiful they look fake. And the prices! I could have people-watched all day." Liz chuckled. "There was everything from underwear to jewelry to fish and flowers. Do you think the vendors charge more to the gringos?"

"Some do. But the locals soon learn who they are and we frequent the vendors who treat us fairly. Now eat up. As soon as we finish, I'll take you to Tonala, where we can shop till we drop. Some of the best artisans in all of Mexico live there. Many work right out of their homes. The village isn't fancy, but it's as close as we'll get to an art and wine festival."

6 | The Happy Wanderer

Goosey, goosey gander,
Whither shall I wander?
Anonymous

"Who are you interviewing this morning?" Liz asked, spreading her toast with mango jam.

"Carol. I met her at bridge. She's sixty-eight and has just returned from an eight-month trip around the world...by herself. What are you going to do?"

"Your neighbor Britt and I are going to take the dogs on a walking tour of the neighborhood." Liz chuckled. "I've never seen so many wrinkles on one little body."

"Britt lies on top of her house and worships the sun god. Curious minds wonder whether she does that in the buff or not." I downed my last sip of coffee and slid off the stool. "Gotta go. I'll be back when I get here."

Carol had taken a table near the kitchen at the new Village Restaurant in Riberas del Pilar, just outside of Ajijic. Dressed in a red-and-white-striped sailor top and white pants, she waved to me as I entered. She reminded me of a quieter, slightly shorter version of Bea Arthur, with her thick gray hair and gentle smile. The waiter brought us each a glass of ice water and handed us two menus—one side in English, the other in Spanish.

Carol ordered *molletes*—a kind of French roll sliced lengthwise down the middle and slathered with refried beans and melted cheese. I decided on Joe's special.

"I want to hear more about your recent adventures, Carol, but first, tell me where you came from and why."

Carol relaxed into her chair. "I'm from Victoria, British Columbia. I came to Mexico originally on a vacation to Mazatlan and fell in love with the country. For the first time in my life I didn't want to go home at the end of my vacation. I did go home, though, and worked another two years." She sighed and rubbed the back of her neck. "I was tired and stressed. I desperately wanted a change of lifestyle. I was fifty-three then, and an administrator for a law firm. I wanted to read all night and not worry about getting up and going in to work the next morning.

"I knew I could never live in a beach resort. That wasn't the real Mexico. So a friend suggested I try Guadalajara, about four hours inland. In February 1985, after falling in love with Guadalajara, I returned to Victoria, gave notice, and moved to Mexico in the middle of July. I didn't know a soul. I'd taken a few Spanish lessons, but they were practically useless." She laughed. "I could order tacos."

"Was that a problem for you in Guadalajara—not knowing the language?"

"No. I found the Mexican people so helpful. I used what little Spanish I had and everyone helped. If I made a mistake, they would gently correct me. I'd joke about it. They knew I wanted to learn and it worked out very well."

"How's your Spanish now?"

"Mediocre."

I consider my *español* mediocre, too. I can get my needs met and understand most of what is said to me, if spoken slowly, but my grammar stinks. With fourteen conjugations, it takes a lot of work, it takes crossing chasms, to become fluent in the language.

"Was it difficult to make friends?" Guadalajara is a city of

8 million people and I knew there wasn't an enclave of expatriates in any one area as there is in Ajijic.

"Easy. Originally I stayed at a little hotel right downtown that was very reasonable. I went to a Unitarian meeting and met some nice people there."

"When you first arrived, what were your fears or anticipations?"

"I had decided to stay one year, regardless of what troubles or hardships there were. I knew there would be adjustments. You can't move to a different country and think it's going to be easy." She looked at me and smiled. "Wrong. After the first year, I was still waiting for problems that never happened. I met wonderful Mexican people and North Americans. Everything just fell into place."

The waiter returned with my cup of coffee and refilled our water glasses. This new restaurant was clean, but bland, lacking the typical bright Mexican colors. Beige walls and beige tablecloths whispered "sedate" rather than shouting "exciting." I wondered if a gringo had chosen the décor and if he thought this was what older expatriates would prefer. I took a sip of coffee and then asked, "How long did you live in Guadalajara?"

"Seven years. I loved the city, but now there's just too much pollution for everyday living. I ended up having bronchitis like I'd had when I was a smoker. Eventually, I decided to move to the Lakeside."

"Had you already made friends down here or did you have to start all over?"

"I started all over again. It seems to me there is about a four-year cycle with the expats I knew. Then they would start moving away—either to other parts of Mexico or back to Gringoland. My move fit in with one of those four-year cycles."

Carol wore small pierced earrings and no other jewelry. Her nails were manicured, but unpolished. She struck me as having a quiet strength. I had the feeling she might be less reserved once we knew each other better. "You retired early. Did you think you had enough money tucked away, that you could live the rest of your life here?"

"I sure hoped so." Her gray-green eyes twinkled. "At that time it was much more reasonable to live here than it is now." She smiled. "For the first four years, I lived on $600 a month and lived very well. I traveled all over Mexico and went to Canada for two months each year."

"And now you're receiving Social Security?"

She wagged her finger at me. "Unh unh. I'm from Canada. I receive money from The Canadian Pension Plan."

"And what do you think your living costs are now?"

"If I include rent and travel, I'd guess between $1200 and $1500 U.S. dollars a month."

"Have you been married? What about kids and grand-kids?"

"I've been married twice and had six children. I've even got two great-grandchildren."

"How did you feel, moving so far away from your family?"

"It wasn't so difficult. In Canada, we were scattered and it was a day's trip to visit any of them. We all worked. We had sort of been weaned from each other. I always knew that the best thing I could do for my children was to teach them how to live their own lives. We're always glad to see each other, then it's time to go home again."

"Do they come down to visit?"

She smiled. "Oh yes."

"What did they say when you told them you were moving to Mexico?"

Carol hesitated a minute. "When I told my mother, she paused a long time and said, 'I guess you know what you're doing.' My children all said, 'Good for you. Way to go, Mom.' I knew my shoes wouldn't be nailed to the floor, and if I didn't like it, I could always go back."

The waiter came with our meals. I put my pad of paper in my lap so he could set down the dishes, and then said to Carol, "This is the pause button on the recorder. When you want to take a bite and not have to talk with your mouth full, just press here. You have the power."

Their special was not as good as Original Joe's in San Jose, but quite a tasty blend of scrambled eggs, spinach, hamburger, and onions. A fruit cup made out of half an orange shell contained pieces of cantaloupe, mango, papaya, pineapple, and watermelon. I was glad I'd chosen what I had, instead of Carol's *molletes*, which didn't look too appetizing. After a few bites, I asked, "What adjustments did you have to make when you moved to the Lakeside?"

"I knew no one when I moved here. It just took a little time to acquire a new circle of friends. I bought my house and met the people next door, who introduced me to other people and it just snowballed."

"I met you at bridge. What else do you do to occupy your time?"

She nodded. "Friends said to me before I left, 'You're a workaholic. You're working sixty hours a week and retirement will be a big adjustment.' " Carol shrugged. "They were wrong. I just put all my efforts into doing nothing." She took another bite of her *mollete*s.

"I know what you mean." I said. "When I moved down here, the only five-year goal I had was *not* to have a goal."

Carol wiped her face with a napkin. "It seems like I'm always traveling. I read. I read a lot. Occasionally I knit or crochet as the mood strikes me. Everyday things take so much longer." Carol chuckled. "When I first got here, I'd run into someone downtown and ask, 'You want to have lunch tomorrow?' If the answer was 'I'm going to the bank,' I'd say, 'Okay then how about the next day?' You could easily plan on four hours to go to the bank and cash traveler's checks." I shook my head in amazement. "It wasn't so bad," she said. "You'd meet people in line and catch up on the local gossip."

"My experience is," I said, "if I get to the utilities offices and banks when they first open, the Mexicans haven't started their day yet and I can quickly get in and out. When I've tried in the afternoons, lines trail outside the building and I say, 'Mañana is good enough for me.' "

I slid my half-completed meal across the table and retrieved my notepad. "You're housesitting now. Why?"

"I sold my house eighteen months ago. I wanted to travel.
I'd always wanted to go to Greece. I was afraid if I waited any
longer, I might never do it." Carol shoved her plate across the
table and leaned back in her chair. "I'm the kind of person who
is always improving my home. I might move this wall here or
add a terrace there. I realized I was putting my long-distance
travel money into the house rather than using it for travel. It
was time to sell the house and complete my dream."

"You sold it furnished?"

"Lock, stock, and barrel. I stored boxes of my personal
stuff at a friend's house."

"Why didn't you rent, since you planned on returning?"

Carol leaned forward, putting an elbow on the table. "A
traveling friend once told me, 'Don't have anything hanging
onto your shirttail.' Now, I'm pretty free to take off. No house.
No kids. No pets. I traveled throughout Mexico for the first
year, before venturing out on my round-the-world trip."

"You didn't find it uncomfortable, being a single woman
traveling alone in Mexico?"

"I learned when I first came here, when I was much
younger, to become the invisible woman." In response to my
raised eyebrows, she said, "I have no eye contact with the
Mexican men. If I do, they might turn around and follow me."
The waiter cleared off our table and refilled my coffee cup.
"Mind you," Carol said with a half smile, "I was fifty then and
in the beach towns."

I nodded, thinking, And quite a looker, too. "Several of
my Mexican friends have said that all Mexican men believe
North American women coming to the beach resorts without
husbands or boyfriends are expecting to get laid."

"That's right," Carol said, chuckling. "The Mexican girls
certainly aren't going to give it to them." She shook her head.
"I've seen gringas come down to Mexico and do things they'd
never consider doing at home."

"Like?"

"Like wearing inappropriate clothing or walking around the downtown area with a bottle of beer in their hand. They're asking for trouble when they behave like that."

I grinned. "Speaking of trouble, how's your love life down here?"

"Nonexistent right now."

I waited. Then Carol shifted in her chair and chewed on her lower lip. "I think the older we get the more difficult it is. We get set in our ways. Maybe it's my personality, but I seem to attract men who want me to take care of them. I've raised my children and I'm finished with caregiving. I'm not looking for someone to take care of me either." A grin played around the edges of her lips. "It would be nice to have someone around to play with, though."

"Have you been involved in any Mexican relationships?"

Carol pushed the pause button on the recorder. I chuckled and then turned the recorder back on. "Okay, let's talk about cultural differences, then."

She thought a moment. "I was at a party of gringos and Mexicans one night. Georgia, the hostess and a married American woman, had invited her Mexican neighbor from downstairs. Carlita was also married and her husband worked in Monterrey. Georgia kept saying to Carlita, 'We'll just have to whip up to Monterrey sometime and surprise your husband. We'll just go and check on him. We'll do this real soon.' Carlita finally burst into tears and Georgia had no idea why. She didn't understand that Carlita's husband had a second family in Monterrey. Everyone knew it, even his wife.

"And there are other cultural differences within Mexican families. Teenagers here are very close to their parents. Both sons and daughters walk around town holding their mother's hand. They don't feel the need to pull away from the family, as do the teens in Canada and the U.S. Our teenagers want to walk ten paces ahead or behind until they reach eighteen or nineteen, when they need to have a parent again."

I laughed. "I decided years ago that teenagers are God's punishment for everything we've done wrong in this life or any other one we may have lived. Maybe I was wrong. Maybe it's just God's punishment for the American and Canadian parents." We laughed loud enough to get the attention of our waiter. I thought a second and said, "Perhaps that's changing here, too. Graffiti has found its way into Mexico big time during the past five years—and I don't think it's being imported. Tell me a couple stories about your travels in Mexico."

"I've taken about ten trips throughout Mexico—either alone or with friends. I never worried about what might happen." Carol chased the ice cubes around in her glass with a straw. "I know so many people who won't travel because they're afraid. I refuse to let fear control my life."

I thought of the recent security meeting held in Ajijic. I've always been very lax about locking up my house. I leave it open with only screen doors shut to keep the flies out. I have ten-foot walls around the property and they give me a false sense of security. There are such things as twelve-foot ladders here. At the meeting with over 500 in attendance, one of the Mexican officials asked everyone in the audience who had been a victim of robbery, to please stand up. I was shocked. It looked like 30 percent of the audience stood. It made me rethink my sloppy security procedures in a hurry. The sound of Carol's voice yanked me out of my reverie.

"Bus transportation has certainly improved while I've been here. On one of my early trips, my friend and I were heading in the general direction of Guanajuato for a few days. We ended up staying three weeks instead. Men got on the bus, lugging live lambs and goats sewn in gunnysacks with just their heads out so their feet couldn't kick around. Or they'd have boxes of chicks or turkeys they were taking home."

I laughed. "The buses I've been on are nicer than the Greyhound buses in the States. They have televisions, restrooms, and room to stretch out. It's a very pleasant drive to the beach on the ETN line. They even provide snacks and beverages."

Carol leaned back, stretching her arms in the air. "That reminds me of a trek to San Miguel—before I spoke much

Spanish. After asking several Mexicans which line to stand in for the bus to San Miguel, my girlfriend and I boarded the bus. Half an hour into the trip, the conductor asked for our tickets. 'You going to San Miguel?' he asked. I nodded. He said, 'Not on this bus.' My friend and I just laughed and decided we'd go wherever the bus was going. Another adventure.

"A while later, the bus stopped and the conductor frantically waved his arms at the two of us, indicating we should get off the bus. We had no idea what was going on. We thought maybe we'd end up on the road, because we'd gone as far as we'd paid for. In a minute, he waved down another bus coming from behind. He told the driver we were going to San Miguel and we'd already purchased our tickets. We switched buses in the middle of the intersection."

I loved these little vignettes. "Not knowing the language presents lots of opportunities for mistakes and misunderstandings, doesn't it?" I asked.

"Oh yes. But they can be new adventures, too." I sensed that a layer of reserve had just melted off Carol and slipped to the floor.

The waiter came to refill our glasses, wondering, I was sure, why we hadn't asked for the check. Only one other table was occupied in the restaurant and we were in no hurry. "During your adventures in Mexico, have you ever run into any problems or unnerving situations on the road?"

"I've never been threatened. I've had my purse slashed twice in the *tianguis* [open-air markets]." She set her glass of water down hard. "One time I was truly frightened. I was driving down from Arizona on the free road and I noticed a blockade ahead of me. Rather than stopping and taking the risk I would be robbed, I just barreled through. I didn't know whether they'd come after me or not, but I wasn't looking back. Then, directly ahead, I discovered the reason for the blockade." Her voice had a breathless quality to it. "A lightweight plane was flying directly toward me. Obviously, he wanted to land where my car was. I pushed the pedal to the floor and barely avoided a crash as he set down behind me."

Carol exhaled slowly. "I don't know what was in that plane and I don't want to know."

"You mentioned when we were off-line that you considered Ajijic a cocoon of gringos. Do you find this comforting or disturbing?"

"Disturbing. The idea of living in Mexico isn't to come down here and have it be a North American community. I love Mexico and the Mexican people."

"Have you thought about moving somewhere else?"

Yes. I've been to Oaxaca twice, but it takes so long to get north in case of an emergency. My mother's still alive," she explained. "And it would be too expensive for the kids to visit." Carol thought a minute. "I lived in Zamora for six months, in Michoacan, teaching English as a Second Language. The kids were wonderful. Only one boy was difficult. He was the only male in the class and wanted all the attention. He thought he should come first. The rest were so well behaved and so willing to work. It was a pleasure. I loved it."

The waiter wandered toward our end of the restaurant, hands loosely clasped behind his back.

"*La cuenta?*" I asked, requesting our check. They never bring it in Mexico until you ask for it. It's considered rude.

"One of the things I've learned down here," Carol said, "is that the Mexicans love humor, and I've discovered a little goes a long way."

"I'm all ears."

"One time I was driving my parents to the airport, and at the *glorieta* [round-about] on Lopez Mateos, I stopped a little too far into the cross-walk. The traffic officer took one look at me and saw dollars. He came to the window and said, 'You're going to have to pay a fine, or I'll take your license and then you can't drive your car until you go to the *transito* and pay.' I knew the routine. I said, 'Isn't there something else we can do?' He put his hands in his pockets and said, 'That's up to you, *Señora.*' I gave him the equivalent of a couple of dollars in pesos. He looked at me and said, '*Señora,* that is not very much money.' I just smiled at him and said, 'For a rich Mexican like you, that's not much money, but I'm a poor Canadian and that's a lot of money to me.' He laughed and said, 'Go on. Go on to the airport.' "

We both laughed. I paid the restaurant bill, and we walked out to our cars. "You've been home two weeks now, Carol. Have you any idea about your next adventure?"

Carol looked like she'd been caught with her hand in the cookie jar. "Yep. Maybe in November I'll head out again."

"Within Mexico?"

"No, I imagine it will be to other parts of the world." Carol put her hand on her heart. "But I'll always come home to Mexico."

"You packed, Liz?" I hollered as I entered my front door.

"Yep. Gee the week has gone by quickly. I'll be glad when I'm retired, so I can stay longer."

"Me, too, girlfriend. Me, too." It thrilled me that Liz was planning to return. I always worried when friends or family came to visit for the first time. Would they love Ajijic? Would they see the beauty I saw? Would they feel the serenity? Why was it important, I wondered, that the people I loved shared my feelings about this place?

"Did you have a good time, Liz?"

"Oh yes. If it weren't for my family, I could definitely see myself living here. I could never move far from my kids."

We loaded her suitcases into the Explorer and headed to the airport.

"I loved Tonala and Tlaquepaque," Liz said. "Unfortunately, most of the things I wanted to buy were big, expensive, and breakable. I'll have to bring bigger suitcases next time."

After our final goodbye hug at the international gate, Liz said, "I want the first book off the press. Signed, of course. Deal?" I smiled and nodded. "I almost feel like I've been part of the book."

"More than you'll ever know, Liz. More than you'll ever know." I waved until she was out of sight, wishing I could be a fly on the wall when Liz first read the book.

Part II:

It Ain't Over Till the Fat Lady Sings

A husband leaves his wife of twenty-nine years; a hospital casts aside a nurse with a silent stroke, penniless; a financial advisor swindles a woman out of her retirement savings late in life. These women pick themselves up, dust themselves off, and find their heartaches transformed into blessings as they discover the joy of living solo in Mexico.

7 | **Another Door Opens**

...running, painting, swimming, fishing, weaving, gardening.
The activity itself is less important than the act of drawing on your own resources.
Barbara Gordon

As she opened the door, the first thing I noticed about Maggie was her perfect little body—the kind that causes my inner green monster to scream, "I hate her!" At least she was dressed for gardening, so I didn't have to envy the easy way she wore the kind of clothes I could only dream about.

A mutual friend had suggested I talk to Maggie, but Maggie had some questions of her own to ask first. I guess I had the right answers, because she gave me a tour of her home and invited me to sit with her at a huge round cement table in the center of an exquisite garden. Hundreds of orchids hung on intricate pine latticework above and around the garden. She showcased them in topless gourds of diverse shapes and colors. The gourds looked as though they had lost their battle with a machine gun.

"Gourds make excellent pots," Maggie explained. "They're inexpensive, and with holes drilled into them, they provide perfect drainage for my orchids." They had a whimsical quality about them. Maggie lit her second cigarette in ten minutes and poured herself an early-morning Pepsi. I opted for water. "I don't do coffee," she explained. "Pepsi is my way of getting a caffeine fix in the morning." She smiled self-consciously and raised one of her winged eyebrows.

Maggie's long blonde hair was streaked with platinum. She wore it parted in the middle with each side combed up above her forehead, then down again, and finally eased back into a ponytail. More interesting, though, was how her eyebrows and the etched lines of her forehead mirrored that same curve. The upper part of her face resembled line drawings of seagulls soaring high above the sea.

I knew Maggie was fifty-four and had moved to Ajijic nearly two years earlier after a painful divorce. I wondered if she'd be willing to talk about it.

She was.

With her head tilted back and eyes focused up at the trellis, Maggie began. "We'd been married twenty-nine years. My oldest son had just graduated from college and the youngest was a freshman. That was four years ago. It was..." She twisted in her chair, inhaled deeply, and finally found the words. "It was unexpected and excruciating." I could tell by her pained expression, some wounds still festered.

"George and I led the perfect life. He opened up a gym, so I put aside my teaching to be his administrative assistant. We built a nice home, bordered on one side by Lake Minnetonka and on the other by a state park. Our tiny town was beautiful—and cold. Like Ajijic, it was home to artists and writers. For decades, we socialized every weekend with the same set of couples.

"After George left, I found myself without a support system. I was an only child, my parents were dead, and our friends were torn between the two of us. The divorce dragged on for two and a half years.

Maggie circled the ashtray with her cigarette. I decided not to interrupt and she continued.

Leaning forward on her elbows, she tapped her fingers on the table. "When I was married, I was a strong, competent woman who could juggle work, husband, children, and social life." Maggie slumped in her chair. "Then, for two years after my divorce, I was immobilized. I stayed in my house with my loom. I couldn't watch TV, go to the movies, or even listen to the radio. The romantic stories and love songs tore me apart. I didn't have enough will to build a new life for myself. Not only had I lost my husband, I'd also lost my job and my friends. I became apathetic." She tapped her cigarette in the ashtray and looked directly at me with only a hint of a smile. "And probably pretty pathetic, too.

"One day my attorney said, 'Maggie, my advice is that you leave this area. If you could live any place in the world, where would it be?'

"The question shook me. I told him, 'The place I love most in this world is Ajijic, Mexico.'

"He looked confused, then asked, 'Where the hell is Ajijic, Mexico, and why would you want to live there?'

"He didn't know I'd been going there for twelve years with the girls. I explained to him Ajijic was a happy place with good memories. I liked the climate and the people were nice."

Maggie looked up at me and smiled. "Of course two of the 'girls' are in their eighties now. Every year the same group of friends headed to Mexico. The wives came to Ajijic while our husbands went fishing on the coast.

"After thinking about my attorney's suggestion, I came back once more with the girls in March, as though nothing was wrong. I didn't talk to anyone about it, but my goal was to find a house to rent."

"You didn't tell your friends? Why?" At first I was surprised, and then I remembered I hadn't told my friends and family until I had made up my mind. I guess it's a protective device. During decision making, I'm more vulnerable to other people's advice and beliefs. Once I've made up my mind, it takes a Mack truck to change it.

Maggie thought a minute. "Why didn't I tell them? Maybe I didn't feel strong enough. I had been through a traumatic experience. They thought I'd come back with them and things would be like they were. I knew things would never be the same. I told them I wanted a day alone to shop."

She stood up and took a deep breath, looking around with satisfaction. "Can you believe I found this house advertised at the grocery store? It was only $450 a month. I rented it for a year."

"Just like that?"

"Yes, just like that. That night at dinner, I toasted to 'my fresh start in Mexico.' The girls were shocked. They didn't think I should stay here by myself. They didn't understand it was worse for me living by myself at home with everybody looking at me and thinking, You poor thing. You poor divorcee.

"After that, my friends began to drop off rapidly. They invested more of their time with my ex-husband. After all, I was leaving and he wasn't." Maggie stubbed out her cigarette and reached for another.

"What did your kids think?"

She smiled. "They were supportive. 'Go for it, Mom,' my oldest said. 'If I were you, I'd do it in a minute.'"

I sensed Maggie's body strengthen as she continued her story. She leaned forward, her back straight and her head cocked at a semi-triumphant angle.

"I went back to Indiana, sold my house, put my finances in order, and decided there was very little I needed to take with me—except my loom. I had taken up weaving to keep my sanity after George left and I think it had become a crutch. I rented a U-Haul big enough to transport the loom and tow my Jeep. My cousin's daughter helped me drive to Laredo, where we stored everything, waiting for a Mexican moving company to pick it up. They would wait for a full truckload before continuing southward.

"During those next two months I survived in Ajijic with one small suitcase of clothes, two table settings, and a teapot. I felt like I was camping out. I had no radio, no loom, no TV.

"Did you have friends that you'd made over the years of visiting?"

"This was spring and the people I'd met here before were

snowbirds. They only came down during the winter."

I nodded.

"I decided to fix the place up. I didn't have a ladder, so I stacked a chair on top of two card tables, and in my underwear, so I wouldn't ruin the few clothes I had, I painted. Purple, yellow, and green. Bright colors. Happy colors."

Maggie's house was indeed bright and happy. Her mastery of color showed in the finished product. "Are you an artist?" I asked.

"Not really. I do some painting and have participated in a couple photo expeditions to old haciendas and hillsides in bloom with wild-flowers. I'm starting to live some of my long-lost dreams. Learning Spanish is another of those." She leaned back and a Cheshire-cat smile crept across her face.

"What?" I asked. Her smile was infectious.

"My youngest son came down for a few weeks in the summer. He speaks Spanish and I was taking lessons. I'd practice in the restaurants. One night when we were out, I hailed the waiter, *'Jabon!'* feeling pretty proud of myself. My son buried his head in his arms and said, 'Oh God, Mom. Don't say another word. You just hollered, "Soap." You should have said, *'Joven!'*'"

"It could have been worse," I said to Maggie, "you could have shouted, *'Jamon!'* calling him a ham."

When we stopped laughing, Maggie added, "Fortunately, the Mexicans are pretty tolerant of our feeble attempts to communicate in their language. They appreciate our trying."

"Besides gardening, weaving, and studying Spanish, what else do you do to keep yourself busy? This must be a big lifestyle change for you."

"Actually, I'm involved in too many things, which is often a problem for new transplants. I volunteer at the library and have taken on responsibility for publishing this year's phone directory. It takes about three days and three nights of my time each week, but I enjoy giving something back to the community."

"You live right smack in the middle of Ajijic," I said. "I

couldn't believe it when I walked into your house. From the street, it looks like a small, dark little Mexican home; but it's huge and light and your garden is fantastic."

A truck cruised down the street, its driver screeching indecipherable political jargon through a loudspeaker. "Don't the village noises bother you?"

"Not anymore. Some of them are really important. When a man yells, *'Agua! Agua!'* it means he's delivering purified water. When a truck comes by rattling tin cans, I know he'll fill my propane tank, and when I hear a whistle, it's time to get my knives out for sharpening. Then there are the dogs howling, the roosters crowing, the kids playing soccer, and the wannabe band next door."

"Are they any good?"

"When they started about six months ago, they couldn't play—or sing—a note. I couldn't hear myself think over the racket, but now they're quite good and my guests enjoy a complimentary live performance with their evening cocktail."

"I'd be awake all night if I lived here," I said. "And I get crabby without sleep."

"The noises you get used to, and after so many years in the quiet of the woods, I treasure the laughter of children and the church bells resonating off the mountains. It's all background music that lulls me to sleep. For me, it's a big part of the charm of living in the village."

The doorbell rang and Maggie excused herself to answer it. A distinguished Mexican gentleman entered. She introduced us and explained that he had come to check on her orchids. "We met at a local meeting of the Guadalajara Orchid Growers," she said. "He'll come back when we're finished with the interview.

"It's important for me to have a mixture of Mexicans and gringos in my life," Maggie said as she returned to the table with Pepsi and water refills.

Unsure if I should poke near open wounds, I asked, "Are you looking for a relationship?"

She took some time before answering. "No. I think I was

hurt so badly that I'm not trusting of men, women, or couples. I'm choosing my friends carefully. I select those with common interests. I'm slowly coming to the realization that I don't need a man in my life. Sure, it's nice to have someone hold you in his arms and say everything's going to be okay, but I'm not mentally or emotionally ready for that yet.

"Here, I'm inventing a social life for myself that includes a lot of alone time. As a single woman, I don't fit in the social cocktail circles anymore. I've learned how much my life is enriched by the Mexican neighbors and friends I have.

"When I had typhoid, they checked on me two or three times a day, bringing food and helping me with chores."

"Isn't typhoid serious?" I leaned forward, curious about her experience.

"It's pretty debilitating. I was in the local clinic for three days while they pumped me full of antibiotics. It took six months for me to regain my energy."

"How do you get typhoid?" I didn't know anyone else who had contracted it.

"You can get it hundreds of ways and it's not as uncommon as you might think. Usually, it's a hygiene issue. Someone touching food after they've gone to the bathroom without washing their hands. It takes about fifteen days to incubate, so by then you've got no idea where you might have come in touch with it."

"Did you consider moving back home then?"

"No. Not then and not two weeks later." Maggie wiggled back in her chair with a victorious smile.

"What happened two weeks later?"

"I had an emergency hernia operation. I limped to the clinic, doubled over in pain. The doctor on duty called ahead to a hospital in Guadalajara, commandeered two kids from the street to help him carry my gurney into the ambulance, and drove me there himself.

"I was drugged up and the ambulance had no air-conditioning. I thought if I didn't die from the hernia, I'd surely melt. I didn't know where I was going or if I should contact my children. They'd told me to get my ass home when I contracted typhoid. But the surgery went fine and I recovered quickly."

"How about insurance, Maggie?"

"I have the national insurance, IMSS. I didn't even use it for typhoid, because the total cost for those three days in the clinic was less than $200. IMSS costs me about $300 a year and they covered all the costs of the hernia operation. I had excellent care."

"But still you weren't ready to go back?"

"Oh no." Maggie raised her arms. "This village has captured my soul. Yes, I still get depressed occasionally, but here I get over it more quickly. The sun shines and people smile. They're happy. I realize how fortunate I am. My standard of living is not even close to what it was in the States, but relatively speaking, I have so much compared to my neighbors."

She noticed the cigarette smoke heading in my direction and lowered her hand below the table. "It's amazing how much beauty they can create out of nothing. Every Mexican has a skill, whether it's carving or sewing or making dolls out of newspapers stained with coffee."

I thought of the beautiful pine-needle baskets I had purchased the previous week from the Tarahumara Indian women in Copper Canyon. They smelled like California forests and reminded me how wonderful simplicity could be.

"For me," Maggie said, as she surveyed her orchids and lowered her voice, "moving to Mexico has been a learning experience, a searching experience, and a growing experience. I've had to learn how to find and fix things by myself. I can't say, 'Honey, get this' and 'Honey, do that' anymore. I've had to wire lamps, paint ceilings, and move seventy-pound pots around. I'm a little person, but with a dash of ingenuity, I can figure out ways to do things. And I'm proud of those little accomplishments."

I thought how different our lives had been when we moved to Mexico—Maggie in a chasm of grief with scanty self-esteem, and me at the pinnacle of my career, believing I could do anything. Yet we'd both ended up in Ajijic to learn lessons about ourselves that needed learning.

"I've also learned more patience," she said. "When something goes wrong, you just have to realize that it can be fixed. It might be today. It might be tomorrow. As a single woman, I know I need to work things out for myself, and eventually I do. Now, in Mexico, I feel stronger than I was even before my divorce. I can do anything and I can do it alone."

We spontaneously broke into a round of "I am Woman," laughing at our lack of singing ability and struggling to remember the words. "When that song first came out," I said, "I used to get up on a table and sing it off-tune...with gusto."

When we finished laughing, I asked her, "Do you believe in serendipity? Can you conceive yet that this difficult divorce was part of a master plan for Maggie?"

She nodded, looking up at the cloudless morning sky. "I'm starting to believe that now. Six months ago I would have said no. But I know I've been given opportunities for personal growth I wouldn't have had if I was still married."

"What's next in your life?"

She puffed up like a peacock. "I've just bought a house. It's not perfect, but it has great possibilities and I think I'm healthy enough now—both physically and emotionally—to take on a major project. I have this nesting urge and I want to fix up something that's my own."

She walked over to inspect one of her resplendent purple orchids, then turned to face me. She scrunched up her shoulders and opened her eyes wide, accentuating the seagull lines in her forehead. "I guess my life's master plan, like this orchid, is blossoming with just a little TLC from me."

8 | **Bag and Baggage**

I hoped that the trip would be the best of all journeys:
a journey into ourselves
Shirley MacLaine

As Chaz opened the gate, I followed her down a narrow path past the front house and into a small courtyard. I struggled to keep up with her long stride. Noodle thin, she wore gray linen trousers and a tailored white blouse. Her frosted blonde, blunt-cut hairdo framed an attractive, yet slightly gaunt, face. Classy lady, I thought.

On one side of the courtyard stood the kitchen and living room. Across the garden, a separate building housed the bedroom and bathroom. An outside bar with three stools was tucked in among the many potted plants and flowers surrounding the courtyard.

Chaz invited me to sit at the bar. Her long, bony fingers shook slightly as she held a lighter to her cigarette. She had a slender neck and steel-gray eyes. Deep grooves on her upper lip betrayed many years of smoking. Chaz pushed her hair behind one ear and, sitting erect, she crossed her legs. "I'm ready."

"Okay," I said, "let's start with when you retired."

"I'm not retired. I'm on sabbatical."

I waited for her to continue. She didn't. "How long is your sabbatical?"

"It ends whenever I feel like going back to Florida."

I looked at the notes I'd taken when I had called to set up the interview. "You've been here two years?"

She nodded and inhaled deeply. "I came to Mexico because I was sick and burned out. I've applied for Social Security disability. If I get it, I stay; if not, I'll have to go back."

Great, more than a one-sentence answer, I thought. This was progress. "What kind of work do you do?"

"I'm an addiction counselor, specializing in the criminal justice system. With a work permit, I'll be able to practice here...on the up and up." Chaz's guttural laugh surprised me. I'd have expected a softer laugh from such a slender person. "I thought there would be a need for my services here in the Ajijic/Chapala area. However, I've discovered that the addicted people have been that way for a long time." In response to the tilt of my head, she added, "If someone's been drunk for fifty years or if a marriage has been unpleasant for thirty years, they're not going to get help. They obviously like it that way." Chaz tap-tap-tapped her cigarette against the edge of the ashtray.

"Have you looked into getting working papers?"

"Yes. But I came with only $4,000 to my name. Papers would cost $1,000, and until I see a market for my services, I'm putting that on hold."

Yikes, I thought, only $4,000. This is either one gutsy broad or a very crazy one. Then I remembered. Most of my friends felt I belonged in one of those camps when I decided to move to Mexico. "If you don't get your disability, you'll go back home?"

"Yes."

"Do you still have a home in the States?"

"No. I sold everything." Chaz's thin lips pulled back into a rueful smile. "I came here with three suitcases and one dog." Two cocker spaniels lay curled up in the shade of a jacaranda tree.

"One?" I asked.

"She had puppies and I kept one."

The sun peeked through the branches of the jacaranda, playing shadows and light across a phenomenal two-story-high mural on the back wall. "That's incredible," I said, pointing to the mural. Brilliant colors swirled about several goddesslike figures intertwined among gnarled trees.

"The owner of this house is an artist. I'm house sitting for him. He completed the mural a couple months ago." Chaz studied the mural for a few seconds. "He's quite talented, isn't he?" I nodded.

"This village is very conducive to creativity. Many artists and writers live here." Chaz hesitated. "Do you want to see some of my own work?"

"Yes, I'd love to." Her shoulders relaxed a bit and she slid off the stool, inviting me to follow her. In a small studio/workroom off the courtyard, she showed me several painted gourds and some handmade stationery.

"When I'm in the mood, I like to do artsy things. I've been consigning some of these to local stores for resale." Chaz cocked her head slightly to one side with a half-proud, half-embarrassed grin. I picked up one of the note cards and envelopes. She had artfully arranged and pressed tiny dried flowers and weeds onto handmade paper.

"These are beautiful, Chaz. You are a very talented lady." I inferred from the slight shrug of her shoulders that the compliment had pleased her.

We headed back to the bar. "Want a beer?" Chaz asked. The hot May afternoon sun blazed overhead.

"I'd love one."

Chaz ducked behind the bar and opened a mini-refrigerator. She placed two opened bottles on the bar and walked in front to climb up on the barstool.

"Thanks." I pressed the cold bottle to my temple. "What were your biggest hopes, when you came to Mexico?"

"I hoped I would start feeling better. I wanted a new perspective. I would be turning fifty here. Although I wouldn't call it a midlife crisis, I didn't want to be in this same career the rest of my life. I hoped I could find another channel for using what I'd learned." She wiped off the top of her bottle with a napkin.

"Would you say those hopes have come true?"

Chaz propped one elbow on the bar. "I haven't found an answer yet. I still have health issues. The language barrier is a problem for me in my line of work. I put myself through six months of Spanish lessons, but didn't do well. Some people have encouraged me to write more." She took a sip of beer and leaned back. "I've decided not to decide what I'm going to do for a while." She laughed. "I guess that's a decision in itself, isn't it?" I nodded.

"You're relatively young, Chaz. How is your social life here?"

"That's the hardest part for me. Being a single woman in my late forties, I've been left out a lot."

"You mean the couple thing?"

She nodded. "Yes. Even groups of older women don't enjoy having younger women around." That hadn't been my experience. "I've also learned that social groups which develop around common activities like bridge or golfing are very tight-knit groups." She pursed her lips. "I feel like I'm on the outside a lot."

"Have you found a dating life here?"

"No, there are no men my age. Most of the retirees are in their mid-sixties and older. Their values and morals are quite different than mine. I'm a feminist. Sixty- and seventy-year-old men are not comfortable with that. They have more traditional values."

She threw her head back and laughed. I sensed a good one coming.

"There are many more quality women here than there are men. Women who move to a Third World country are generally independent, fully expecting to take care of themselves. Men come here, I think, looking for someone to take care of them. And at a ratio of ten women to one man, the odds definitely favor them.

"Men typically have better retirement benefits, too. I look for leadership qualities in men. I don't see those qualities here and they don't enjoy the arts like I do." She looked at me for my reaction. "As a whole, I graphically call them the belch, fart, and scratch group." We both had a good belly laugh.

"Have you integrated at all into the Mexican community?"

Chaz pursed her lips. "The Mexicans are very pleasant, kind, and gentle. It's nice to walk on the street and say, *'Buenos dias'* or *'Buenas tardes.'* She chuckled. "On the bus, if someone has too many kids to handle, I'll put my arms out and they'll hand me one. Then I'll keep the child until they reach their destination." She tucked her hair behind her ear.

"But integrated? Not really. I'm single. I don't have children. We don't have much in common. This culture has different expectations of a woman than the U.S. does. In Mexico, a woman alone is questioned."

"Why do you think that is?"

"I think it's because of role differences. Roles are defined very clearly here, and they are very muddied in the States." Chaz grinned and tapped her cigarette on the ashtray. "One time I went into a bar filled with Mexican men. Everyone turned to look. I think they expected me to ask a question and leave, but when I sat down and ordered a drink, the place stood still. A Mexican woman would never do that. They question our morals. You have to be careful not to get a reputation.

"Another day, I was cleaning up the grounds. I spent hours dragging banana leaves and weeds out of the garden. When I began, there were a few Mexican women sitting on a doorstep across the street, watching me. When I finished, the whole street was filled with Mexican women sitting on their doorsteps, watching me." Chaz exhaled slowly and purposefully. "The moral of the story? This is improper work for a woman. This is man's work."

I chuckled, picturing the scene, and I wondered: Did Chaz come to Mexico to escape something or to find something? How did she survive? Surely her $4,000 nest egg had been used up in two years. What did she do to fill her time? She had an almost visible wall around her, and I wasn't sure how invasive I should—or could—get.

"Let's get back to your health issues, if I may." Chaz squirmed in her seat.

"Do you have health insurance?"

"No."

"Neither in the States nor here?"

"None."

"How do you deal with that?" Jeez, I thought, sick, and with neither insurance nor money.

"I just don't go to the doctor. It's the way poor Mexicans deal with illness. You get sick and you either get well or you die. Period."

We both laughed, not because it was funny, but to break the tension. I felt I needed to change the subject for a while, although I still hadn't found out what her health problem was. I was beginning to think it was stress related, rather than cancer or some other disease. "How did you find out about Ajijic?"

"I had friends who lived here in the Racquet Club—that new upscale development west of Ajijic. They kept encouraging me to visit. 'You can come here and live cheaply. You can work here,' they said. I spent two weeks here. I should have done more homework. That snapshot I got was clearly not the reality of living in Mexico—at least not my reality." She tapped her cigarette again. "My friends are quite wealthy."

"Until your disability is settled, you have no monthly income?"

"Zero."

"You have no work permit and therefore can't practice your counseling—on the up and up." We both smiled. It's risky business in Mexico to work without a permit. If someone reports you, you can be deported. "So what does it cost you to live each month and how do you earn it?"

"I housesit and provide in-house caregiving. I cared for one eighty-year-old lady twenty-four hours a day, seven days a week. I had no life of my own. It was unacceptable. And I'm

starting these little side businesses." She indicated the stationery and hand-painted gourds with a wave of her hand toward
the studio.

Chaz thought a minute. "Without rent and without a car, I
get by on three or four hundred dollars a month."

"Whew. That must be tough."

"Not so bad. I've taken advantage of all the things that are
here. I buy used clothing from the consignment stores. I shop
for fresh fruits and vegetables from the local market. We
socialize at each other's homes, rather than going to
restaurants, or I meet friends for a cup of coffee. You can
create a comfortable existence without much."

"Okay, Chaz, let's put some of your training and experience to use. What advice would you give women thinking of
moving to Mexico?"

"My first suggestion would be that they deal with their
own emotional issues before coming here. The support sys-
tems they had in the States, they will not have here." She
pushed her hair behind her ear again. "In other words, clean
your house before you come. The expectation is that it's going
to be very exciting and new here. It is for a while, but in time it
will become mundane just like everything was at home.

"I've talked with women who've come here because they
think they can afford to live here. Yes, it's cheaper, but you
can't walk across the street to see your grandchildren. Loneli-
ness can become a major issue. I think you have to be a very,
very strong woman." I flexed my biceps and then flashed my
pearly whites and winked. Chaz rolled her eyes. "No, I'm not
talking physically. I'm talking emotionally and spiritually. No
matter how many wonderful people you meet here, at night
when you shut the door, if you don't have personal strength,
you might feel very much alone."

We both turned to watch as a swallow swooped by us and
disappeared under the eave. The bird carried a beak full of mud
under a curved roof tile. "Swallows make such a mess," I said,
"but I've had them outside my home office for three years and
I love to watch them build their nests, feed their babies, and

teach them how to fly. What's a little poop on the patio?

"What else?" I asked, putting us back on track.

Chaz thought a moment. "Don't come here expecting a 180-degree change in your life. You're still bringing yourself with you."

"For myself," I said, after taking the last swallow of beer, "I had to answer the question, Was I running away from something or toward something?"

"Yes, that's a good question. Whether you're coming here in the middle of your life or in later years, what are you coming for?" Chaz looked up at the sky. "I came because I had no idea what I wanted to do and because physically I wasn't well. I thought coming here would give me some down time to heal and make some decisions."

"How long had you been divorced before you moved to Mexico?"

"Eighteen years."

"So you didn't have to get used to living alone."

She shook her head.

"I interviewed another woman who gave up a thirty-year career, a twenty-year relationship, and a torrid affair to move down here."

Chaz whistled. "As a counselor, I know that puts her way off the stress scale."

"It should have, but I think the serenity she found here— she was from New York City—more than compensated for the stress of so much change."

"That's a good point," Chaz said. "Making a life change and coming to a Third World country doesn't provide the answer for most people, but it gives them a different environment in which to seek the answers."

"I resemble that remark! I knew I was on a journey searching for something." I took a deep breath. "I don't know that I've found the answers yet, even after three years, but that's okay, because I'm enjoying the journey."

Chaz sat up straight and leaned forward. "Right. One needs to be strong and adaptable. Because it *is* a journey, and if you're open to it, it can be exciting. If you come thinking you're going to bring everything with you..."

I interrupted. "Be more specific."

"Fears, wants, needs. Everything you're not comfortable with. You come into a new environment with all the old baggage. That's like moving from Des Moines to San Francisco. Nothing important will change."

Roosters crowed incessantly in the lot behind us. "How do you sleep with those roosters so close?" I asked.

"We have roosters, pigs, and donkeys. It's nothing compared to the sounds of the inner city where I worked in Florida—fire engines, sirens, gunshots." Chaz stood, stretching her back and nodding her head in the direction of the clamor. "On Friday, that rooster flew over my wall. The dogs chased the rooster. I chased the dogs. It was a hoot."

"And the rooster was returned safe and sound?"

"Yep. It seems there's always something interesting happening in the village." She picked up both bottles and put them in a crate behind the bar.

"Last question, Chaz. Has living in Mexico changed you in any way?"

"Hmm. Yes, I think it has. My values have changed. I valued myself in the States by my credentials. Here, those don't matter. Now I stand back and look at myself, not just seeing this professional person but trying to see who I really am." Chaz stubbed her cigarette out, creating concentric circles in the ashes. "For me, this is a process. I guess I'm just beginning to learn who I really am."

9 | Life in a Treehouse

"Toto, I've a feeling we're not in Kansas anymore."
from The Wizard of Oz

Penny met me at her front gate and led me beyond the main house to a narrow wrought-iron staircase, which led up to a second-story deck. She twirled in a circle, a short-sleeved orange and red flowered muumuu swirling about her. Waving an arm behind us, she said, "This is my humble abode. I call it my tree house."

Her charming studio apartment perched atop a single-family home. She had decorated her home, consisting of a small kitchenette, bathroom, and combination living/bedroom, with sunny colors. The living room opened onto the deck through sliding glass doors. "And out there," she said, turning around to face the tall trees and the lake, "my view of the world and my joy in life."

This was a perfect day in Villa Nova, an older neighborhood just west of Ajijic. Cumulus clouds cavorted across the azure sky, serenely reflected in the lake below. Penny brought out cookies and lemonade and then settled into an ample deck chair. Short reddish-blond curls framed her face, and large glasses accentuated fine laugh lines around her eyes.

"You're happy here, aren't you, Penny?" I felt the positive

energy she radiated.

She beamed. "I came here from Ontario six years ago when I was fifty-seven. This treehouse was never part of my life's plan. But then neither was living on a shoestring in the middle of Mexico. I intended to live in the large house below with more of what I considered creature comforts. It didn't turn out that way, but I wouldn't trade one day of this life for one day of the life I left behind."

Penny took a deep breath and her effervescent voice softened. "My mother died a year before I moved here. It was a long, arduous death and I was the sole caregiver. I also had seven-day, twenty-four-hour responsibility for a senior citizen residence in our small hometown."

She added, almost parenthetically, "I had been a registered nurse most of my life. When Mom passed away, I felt alone. My marriages had been unsuccessful and I have no children or siblings. My heart needed some repair. Maybe my soul did, too." Penny rubbed her thumb and forefinger under the nosepiece of her glasses and sighed. "I was a caregiver who had no more care to give. My self-diagnosis was an acute case of stress."

Her shoulders drooped and I could almost see the weight of that responsibility sitting on them. "And what does a nurse prescribe for herself to cure such a disease?" I asked.

"Actually, my director handed me the best prescription. 'Take some time off,' he said. 'Heal yourself.' And do what? I wondered. I felt like a ninety-pound mom must feel after lifting a car off her child. Somehow she has the strength, the adrenaline, to do what she must do and then she collapses. I'd depleted my emotional resources helping Mom die with dignity, and nothing remained for my staff, the residents, or myself."

"Penny, I'm sorry. I hope you followed his advice and took care of yourself."

Out of context, she chuckled, evidently recalling another moment. "I'll tell you the story. Providence intervened. One day I rushed through my front door just in time to pick up the phone. 'Penny Martin?' It was an unfamiliar voice. 'My name is

Vincent Raymond, from the law firm of Raymond, Marwick & Tanner. Your friend Amy Singer left the sum of $2,000 to you in her will. Her instructions are: "Penny, please use this money to celebrate our birthdays." Can you come to the office and pick up the check? I'll need your signature.'

"Amy and I had celebrated our identical birthdays for years by taking trips together. She had wanted our next trip to be Guadalajara. I was stunned. How could I go alone? How did she expect me to celebrate her birthday when she was dead?" Penny raised her palms skyward in supplication.

"Perhaps it was her life she wanted you to celebrate?"

"Yes. After a lot of soul searching, I understood that. Our birthdays were only three weeks away and my stress level continued to mount.

"As it happened, another friend, Shirley, decided to go with me. Concern about this trip, coming on the heels of both my mother's and Amy's deaths, had glued me to an emotional seesaw. One minute I was crying and the next my heart soared over adventures yet unknown, but in some way anticipated.

"The travel agent suggested we stay in Ajijic rather than Guadalajara. 'It's a kinder, gentler place,' she said. 'You can take the bus into Guadalajara for day trips.' It sounded like the right thing to do. With the purchase of those tickets, I had unwittingly taken the first step in my life's new direction and there would be no turning back."

Very much like my dream, I thought. A new land and a new life. Penny scooted toward the edge of her chair, as though anticipating her own story. "We arrived in Ajijic after nightfall. In the morning, I opened the curtains and gasped. After months of Canadian snow and slush and gray and brown, I looked across a sparkling blue pool and saw lush green mountainsides beyond the lake. I opened the windows and inhaled deeply. 'Hey, Shirley,' I said, shaking her blanketed foot, 'look! I don't think we're in Canada anymore.'

"Shirley stumbled to the window, looked at me, and started laughing. 'Penny, I'm not sure, but you look like you're bewitched.' Tears threatened to spill out and I could only nod.

"We met other Canadians and Americans on the streets and in the restaurants. They talked incessantly about what a great place this was to retire. The seed of an idea began to germinate. Maybe I wouldn't have to work nine more years. Perhaps I could afford to live here until my retirement funds were accessible. That seed took root, spreading slowly throughout my subconscious."

"Yes!" I said. "That's exactly how it happened with me. First it was a notion, then an idea, then a burning desire."

"I love the mountains here," she said, looking northwest. "When I first got here, the emerald green mountains reminded me of Oz." She laughed and paused. "One afternoon," she continued, "I told Shirley that I felt like the Cowardly Lion who had asked the Wizard for courage. I'd need more than I had if I was going to follow this inexplicable yearning and march down that yellow brick road to Mexico."

Still chuckling, Penny continued. "Shirley tapped her pencil on my head and said, 'Penny, you're not the Lion, you're the Scarecrow—in need of a brain!' She wasn't the last person to tell me I was crazy."

I smiled and nodded. "My experience has been that people fall into one of two camps. Either they think I'm crazy or they're jealous as hell!"

Penny almost choked on her lemonade.

"Go ahead, Penny. You've arrived in Ajijic. The weather is beautiful. Shirley thinks you're crazy, and then?"

"On Thursday, we joined a weekly tour of homes. It was a fundraiser for the School for the Deaf. The locals welcomed us into their breathtaking haciendas with acres of manicured gardens. The last home on the tour was small but incredible. Designed and decorated by a well-known modern Mexican architect, the two-bedroom, two-bath villa sparkled with bright colors. A two-story curved wall, painted in mottled purple and pink, dominated the living room. The home snuggled into the hillside with a lake view that tugged at my heartstrings. It offered the kind of outside-in feeling I love. I said to Shirley, 'I could be very happy living in this house.'

"Shirley rolled her eyes upward and shook her head in disbelief. 'Lucky for you,' she said, 'it's not for sale.'

"I was awake all night. Numbers and sketches and pros and cons danced across pieces of paper covering our desk and part of the sofa. By the time Shirley woke up, I said, 'You'd better get us both a cup of coffee, because you're about to play devil's advocate to my impossible dream.'

"I rambled for the next few hours while Shirley played her role to the hilt. My biggest concern was money. Mom's house had been appraised during probate, and with the equity in it, I thought I could afford to buy a house here and have enough left to live on until my social security kicked in. I was tired of senior caregiving, and although Shirley did her best to talk me out of this 'romantic fiddle-faddle,' she failed. Friday morning I put her on the plane back to Ontario.

" 'I've been in touch with my office,' she had explained, 'and have to get back sooner.' Maybe she was getting fed up with me. I'm sure I was acting like a kid at her first circus. Shirley probably saw me as having cotton candy smeared all over my hands and face and she didn't want to get sticky."

"Good imagery, Penny. Speaking of sticky hands—can you please bring out a couple of napkins? These cookies are good, but the chocolate is melting." While she did that, I leaned forward against the railing, inhaling the smells of the woods and watching the birds play in the branches. Penny's house felt secluded, although it really wasn't. The architect had done a good job.

Penny returned with napkins and I asked, "And after Shirley left?"

"After she left, I met Pete, a local Realtor. The third house Pete showed me was on the same hillside as the one on tour. This one needed lots of work, but it was for sale. And the view... I stood on this very deck the day he showed me this very house and I felt a layer of stress melting away. I wrote Pete a check for the 10 percent deposit. We faxed an offer and the owners accepted. 'Big breaths, Penny,' I told myself. 'Big breaths.' "

"You're not the only one who bought impulsively, Penny. I bought a house on my third day here. My real estate agent friend says about 50 percent of the folks who come down with no intention of buying actually do. Maybe it's something in the air."

Penny's laughter sounded like the gurgling of a stream. "I figured all I had left to do was quit my job, sell Mom's house, pay the other 90 percent, remodel my new home, and…I had no idea how many hundreds of other details would be involved in such a major move. I was excited—the blow-your-skirt-up kind of excitement that had eluded me for so long. I felt wild and crazy."

She put her elbows on the table and leaned forward. "I phoned my friends and my boss and told them I was moving to a mountain village in the center of Mexico. 'Penny, you're crazy,' my boss said. 'You've gone completely berserk. People do a lot of homework before buying a house, any house, let alone one in a Third World country.'

I pursed my lips, thinking that her boss was right, and that people like Penny and me probably seemed a bit off-center to the general population. I shook my head and thought, Probably?

"They were right," Penny continued. "I was acting completely out of character. My gut said go for it, and I did. It was just that simple. And just that crazy. Those baby steps I was taking earlier had grown into full-fledged Olympic strides."

She lifted her eight-year-old Shiatsu onto her lap. "We weren't crazy, were we, Baby? The dog's real name," she explained, "is Babylon." Baby reached up to lick her mistress's face. Penny topped off our lemonades and leaned back in the breeze, eyes closed, a serene smile playing across her lips.

"I'm trying to put myself back in that time and place," she said, "because it felt like the heavens had been wrapped up and presented to me on one of Mom's sterling silver platters. Then I started to worry about what I'd do with all that stuff back home, generations of furniture, all antiques, and the china and crystal. In retrospect, letting go of those heirlooms was the hardest thing I ever had to do, and probably taught me one of the most important lessons in my life."

My ears perked up. Lessons interested me. Most of the women I had interviewed had learned significant lessons about themselves after moving to Mexico.

Penny shoved her glasses higher on her nose and wriggled in her seat. "As fate would have it, two days before I left Ajijic, I was waiting on the highway for a bus to take me to Chapala. This old man in a beat-up van offered me a lift. I accepted because life was wonderful and his plates were from Ontario. His name was Bert.

"We started talking about Canada and home and I couldn't shut up about my house and Villa Nova and the lake and how on earth I'd get my prized possessions down here. Bert said he was heading to Ontario in the summer and would be glad to bring back a load for me.

"A load, I thought. One load? That would certainly force me into making some tough decisions. Could I live without those things? Did I even want them? I wasn't sure, but I'd have some time to work it out before Bert arrived in late June."

"Another bit of serendipity?" I asked.

Penny nodded. "Baby and I were sure happy to see each other when I got back to Ontario. Then, as though the Wicked Witch of the West had cast an evil spell on me, things began to turn sour. The real estate market had softened considerably since we last had the house appraised. I'd be getting 30 percent less than I'd anticipated—if the house sold at all.

I called my accounting firm to see about borrowing against my retirement fund, only to find out my portfolio had been mismanaged along with those of several other customers of the firm, and I'd lost most of my investment. There seemed to be no legal recourse. I had a panic attack. I screamed. I yelled. I cried. I'd already resigned from my job. I sat around for weeks in a deep depression.

"Yes, I should have paid attention," she said, glancing at me with a don't-*you*-start-in-on-me look. "But for the two years Mom was ill, I didn't.

"The house sold. I wasn't sure if that was good news or bad. Baby helped make the decision. It was raining outside. I wanted her to go out and relieve herself. She resisted going into the cold and wet. I didn't like it either. We wanted to go to Mexico. Two months later, we arrived.

"I didn't know anything about crossing the border, but Bert did. He was a gray man with gray hair, gray face, and gray clothes. He looked much older than he was, and of course he didn't have the right papers to bring my things in duty-free. But he said he knew the tricks. My Ajijic friends and I laughed when he told the story about how he'd managed the Mexican border crossing.

" 'At the border,' Bert told us, 'we got that darn red light. So if that guard had a fight with his wife in the morning or was hung over, we was at risk of having everything taken out of the van and trailer. I closed my eyes tight and grabbed at my chest. "My heart," I whispered to my grandson, but loud enough for the guard to hear, "it's my fool heart."

" 'Jake, he's my grandson, he froze his eyes into the worst fear you could imagine and said in a cracked voice that was half boy, half man, "Gramps, I'll drive. We need to get you to the Vet hospital in Guadalajara." That guard looked a bit pale himself and waved us through with a "Godspeed." '

"Anyway, the treasures Bert hauled down arrived intact and on time. I wish I could say the same for the house I bought. It had more than a few problems. I had sent my contractor half of the remodeling fee so the work would be done when we got here. The renovations that were done were wrong and at least half weren't completed. Of course, to fix the problems, he needed more money—money I didn't have. I learned never to have work done when I'm not here to supervise."

"Amen!" I said. "Lesson number one. It's the squeaky wheel that gets the grease here. They have this inborn need to make whoever is in front of them happy. I think it's part of their living in the present moment. They don't worry about how unhappy you're going to be next month when you come back until that day. Also, with the language barrier, they often think they understand what we want when they really don't. I can't tell you how many things I've had to redo. Anyway, I digress. What did you do then?"

"I didn't see any other way but to put my dream home on the market, figuring I'd recoup the $125,000 I'd invested in it and find something cheap to rent. Surprise! The house was valued at significantly less than that. There's something about being a woman alone down here. We're so trusting and it's easy to be taken advantage of—by slick gringos as well as Mexicans. I guess Shirley was right—I had too much courage and not enough brains."

I shook my head. "It's not so much a matter of brains, Penny, but of experience and of doing your homework. It's easy to be too trusting down here. It's all so magical and you want it to be that way. It's as if magic and business don't mix well. As an alternative, did you consider working here?"

"I checked into nursing, but without fluent Spanish, I couldn't work here. Summoning up the last of my waning courage, I spent what was left in the bank to build this small studio on top of my house. I rent out the house below for $650 per month, U.S. dollars. That's the shoestring I live on now."

"That's not a lot. You must have learned to eat like the locals."

"Yes, but I'm a far better person because God didn't let me plan out my own life. I've had to pare down a lot. Things, I've found, aren't nearly as important as people. See that silver coffee pot? It's been in my family for generations. I couldn't bear to leave it in Canada. I've never used it once. I should sell it. I could spend the money on something useful.

"More important, though, is that I've stopped judging others based on their wealth or social position. I must have been a snob in Canada. Here, my friends and I accept each other regardless of our financial means. It's been a humbling lesson for me—an important one. What I have now is good health, good friends, and the time to enjoy them. It doesn't cost much, you know, to sip lemonade with a new friend and watch the clouds drift across the sky."

I turned off the recorder and Penny laughed, a raucous, infectious laugh that started in her belly and bubbled up inside her. She was obviously pleased with herself. "What?" I asked, laughing with her in spite of myself.

"In addition to the brains Shirley hoped the Wizard would give me, and the courage I thought I needed...well, he must have thrown in some extra heart for the Tin Man in me, too."

10 | Stretching the Bucks

"What, me worry?"
MAD magazine

I opened my front door to see Britt brushing her fingers through her thick white hair. "This damned cement dust never ends," she explained. Don't ever stay in your house when they're putting on a new roof." Britt raised a bottle of white wine as a sly smile crept across her face.

"At least it's white," I said. The one time I'd been at her house, in an attempt to rescue a glass from being toppled by her dog's tail, my shirtsleeve had caught the rim of another goblet and spilled red wine onto her new rug.

Britt winked. "I really wanted to get merlot."

"Hunh unh," I said. "It wouldn't go with your pretty white tennis outfit." I waved her into my living room and shut the door behind her. "I'll get some glasses for that wine."

As I followed Britt to the patio, wine glasses and a bowl of Ritz Bits in hand, I remembered hearing her nickname, Q-Tip, from a mutual friend. Mexicans love their nicknames. They call my painter *"Palillo"*—toothpick. Jose must have been very thin as a child. The Mexicans create nicknames for us gringos, too, but they never use them to our faces. I wondered what they called me.

Extremely wrinkled, Britt's deeply tanned skin hugged her minuscule frame. She reminded me of a leathery old guide who'd led a group of us on a climb up the Egyptian pyramids. Her thin body, topped with that short crop of white hair, must have led one of the locals to think of a 'Q-Tip.'

We sat down at the glass-topped table on my patio. "Wow!" Britt said. "I love your backyard. It's really grown since I saw it two years ago. It reminds me of an old English garden."

"Thanks. I give my gardener a free hand. He brings over cuttings from other folks' gardens and takes some of mine back to them. It reminds me of wildflowers. I love the butterflies and birds the flowers attract." I thought about my gardener for a second. "Martin is very young, very shy, and very good."

I selected a chair opposite Britt, poured the wine, and began. "Tell me who you were before you moved to Mexico."

Britt pulled one knee up to her chest and balanced her glass on top of it. "I managed doctors' offices, mostly setting up their payables and receivables. I did that for twelve years. Before that, I was married twice and had three children." It always amazed me when people defined who they were by their job. At least she included her role as wife and mother. Not fair, Blue, I told myself. You did that for years, too.

I brought my attention back to Britt as she continued. "I'm originally from Norway..."

"I'm half Norwegian," I interrupted. "But how the hell do you get so tan in a Norwegian body? All I ever do is burn and peel, burn and peel."

"You're probably better off. I'm a sun worshipper. You've seen the *mirador* on top of my house?" I nodded. "I spend a lot of time up there reading and basking. From my rooftop deck, you can see the lake and the mountains. Since the dogs have learned to climb the narrow circular staircase, they generally join me up there." Britt lit a cigarette and inhaled deeply before continuing.

"I didn't work at all until I was forty-one. Then I went to a nurse's aide school and worked in convalescent homes and acute hospitals until I started managing the doctors' offices. When one of the doctor's wives decided she wanted to come back to work, I was laid off. I was sixty-seven then."

"Hadn't you considered retiring before that?"

"No, never. I had to support myself, and I couldn't imagine not working, or waking up in the morning and wondering what I'd do that day. It's my type-A personality. After I was laid off, I tried to get another job, but I ran smack dab into age discrimination." Britt sneered and jutted out her chin.

"Were you getting Social Security benefits then?"

"Yes. I started taking benefits at sixty-two, and that was the biggest mistake I ever made. They took 33 percent of everything I made over $11,000 a year. Because I didn't start working until I was forty-one, I didn't have any retirement funds. So there I was, unemployed and trying to live on $735 a month in Southern California. My kids subsidized me with an extra $250 each month, but $985 still didn't cut it there."

"That's why you moved to Mexico?"

Britt nodded. "I came down to visit a friend of mine who was teaching at the University of Guadalajara during the summer. Her roommate had returned to the States and there was an empty bedroom. She said, 'Come and stay with me for two weeks and help me drive back to Arizona.' I thought, Why not? What else do I have to do?

"One day I took the bus to Ajijic and thought it was kind of nice. One of the agencies had advertised a small furnished house for rent and I took it."

"Just like that? What did your family and friends think?"

"Humph. They thought I'd lost it and it was time to white-jacket me." Britt lowered her foot to the ground, leaned forward on the table, and laughed—a gruff, raspy laugh. "In the middle of the argument, my youngest said to her siblings, 'Give it up. You know Mom's not going to change her mind.'

"I've lived back and forth between Norway and the U.S. and spent a couple years in Italy and Japan. Moving to another country was no big deal." Britt smiled, deep wrinkles traveling up her face. "I put what stuff I could fit in my little yellow Sprite and headed south. I stored the rest at a friend's house. My son was going to drive it all down at Christmas. Then he fell in lust and went to Louisiana instead." She shrugged her shoulders. "Can't compete with lust."

"So you moved into a furnished rental? In the village?"

"Yes, I took a six-month lease. It was a nice enough place, but I didn't like the neighborhood. As soon as I could, I sublet that apartment and found the house I'm living in now. Of course, it was unfurnished, but at $275 a month, the price was right. I furnished it by scouring the consignment and junk stores."

"It's a two-bedroom, one-bath, right?"

"It is now. It had a huge living room and a huge dining room; I converted the dining room into a second bedroom. There was a pool, but the motor didn't work, so my gardener filled it up with dirt. *Voila!* Now it's a nice garden. Bless his soul, he only charged me 800 pesos."

"In California, landlords fuss if renters put a nail in the wall."

Britt shook her head. "It's different down here. You can do pretty much whatever you want in a rental. I have friends who've installed automatic garage door openers, put in additional closets, and added a *mirador.* The only problems landlords are responsible to take care of are health or safety hazards. Other than that, renters are on their own."

"Have you found you can live comfortably on your income here?" I asked.

She didn't hesitate. "Yes. I eat out a couple of times a week at a reasonably priced restaurant. I don't have a big appetite, so I don't spend much on food. My little car gets forty-eight miles to the gallon." Britt scowled. "When some idiot hits it on the highway, then that gets a little expensive. I buy material and have my clothes made. My propane is 100 pesos per month, the electricity is 100 pesos for two months, and…"

"One hundred pesos?" I interrupted again. "Mine is 800 pesos. I must be doing something very wrong."

"Or having things like a washer and dryer, garage door opener, water pressure system, dishwasher…" Britt rolled her big blue eyes as though to say she had little empathy for my problems.

"I also do some work to provide extra money for myself. I worked at a nursing home for two and a half years and now I'm a critter sitter." As though on cue, my poodle, Maurice, jumped into her lap. Britt rubbed him behind his ears and set him down.

"Did you need a work permit?" I asked.

"Probably, but I never got one. It's a pain in the derriere, and I didn't want to do it. I was making only 1,200 pesos a month. That's only 10 percent of 1,200 dollars. This was just for extra money—to get my car fixed or to take a trip home." Britt stretched her arms over her head. "In three years, I've only gone home to California once. I drove."

"Do your kids visit?" I asked.

"My son and my youngest have been here." Britt shrugged her shoulders. "The kids are involved in their own careers. They're busy and there's not much here for younger folks. My son—he's lived in Third World countries before—is a bachelor. He thinks Mexico is the cat's pajamas." She leaned back and blew a smoke ring into the clouds. "I have to live my life and they have to live theirs."

"Have you considered living anyplace else?"

"I'm considering Baja."

"Why?"

"Because it's one hour from home. By this time next year, all my family will live near San Diego. As I get older, I realize I want to see my family more than once a year." Britt's face lit up. "I have a grandson that I'm totally bananas about. He came down and hated every minute of it. That was before the Toblandia water slides, and there was nothing for him to do."

"Do you ever think about moving home?"

"No. I can't afford to live the way I'd like to live in the States. I could probably find one of those government-assisted dark little apartments with a bunch of other little old ladies."

She stubbed out her cigarette. "I have no intention of doing that. The cost of living in Ensenada is about the same as here. Rent is higher, but other things are less expensive. I need to go there and look."

I chuckled. "So, if you don't like to spend your time with little old ladies, how do you spend it?"

"I'm an early riser. Sometimes by 8 a.m., I've played two sets of tennis. I do this critter-sitter business, my own house-work, and some gardening. I've taken in five street dogs, but two decided life was better elsewhere and left. I cook for the dogs and play with them…"

"You cook for your dogs," I asked.

"Research I've have gathered from the Internet and from holistic vets is pretty damning of the packaged pet foods. It's not difficult," Britt added. "My dogs love the food and their health has greatly improved. I use one part protein mixed with two parts carbohydrate and two parts vegetables."

"What else do you do with your day?"

"I read. Just garbage novels, but I enjoy them. I watch my favorite TV programs. I don't know how, but the days just fly by. I can't believe that on August 6th, I will have been here three years. Oh, and I have a ninety-five-year-old male friend that I visit and take out for rides. He was one of my patients at the nursing home. I see him twice a week."

"You're a good man, Charlie Brown," I said. "How about challenges? Do you face any living here?"

"Sure, but the biggest challenge I face is me. I need more patience than I have. I need to learn that mañana doesn't mean tomorrow, it just means 'not today.' You can't scream at the Mexicans. We're guests in their country. If they don't come, fine. I just go about my business. I can't sit around all day wait-ing for them." She thought for a minute. "I also hate the way they treat their animals. And it infuriates me they won't get them neutered when it's free. I hate seeing puppies abandoned.

"On the other hand, I love the climate, the birds, the don-keys and horses clippety-clopping by."

"How's your *español, Señora?*" I asked.

"Not bad. I handle my grocery shopping, order from restaurants, and talk with my gardener in Spanish. It was easier for me to learn than for some, since I'm already bilingual in Norwegian and English. I think it's a big mistake for people to come down here and not take lessons."

Britt reached over and dipped her hand into the Ritz Bits bowl.

I asked, "If you had a friend considering moving down here, what advice would you give her?"

"Hurry up and do it!" Britt slapped her hands on her knees. "Let's face it. Someone in my financial situation has one hell of a good life here, compared to living in the States. Once in a while I have a haircut. It costs fifty pesos. In California, I pay ten times that." She leaned back in her chair. "But there are some people who should never come down."

"Like?" I asked.

Britt held up her fingers one by one.

"Number one: people who look at a dirty diaper in the street and say the town is filthy.

"Number two: people who can't stop and smell the roses.

"Number three: people who want everything to be like it is in the States or Canada.

"Number four: people who don't appreciate different cultures.

"Number five: nasty people. They give the rest of us a bad name.

"How do the Mexican's treat you?" I asked.

"Wonderfully. My butcher calls me *Reyna*—the queen. I think that's because I speak their language, and maybe because of my age. They really respect us older folks. Even if you say something totally wrong in Spanish, they appreciate your trying."

"Any other words of wisdom?"

"Yes. Women looking for a man shouldn't come down. If you don't like yourself, you can't live alone. If you can't cope, stay home. It'll take awhile to get a network going. Plan for six months to adjust. Don't expect your neighbor or doctor to do things for you. This is an adventure. Be adventurous. You only get one time around."

"Last question, Britt. Are you ever afraid here?"

"No. I refuse to live in fear. I don't act stupidly. I tried driving home once from Guadalajara at night. No lights, no white lines, pedestrians walking across the highway, and black cows. It's too dangerous."

Britt's face lit up with a wicked grin as she downed her last sip of wine and put out her second cigarette. "Here's a story for you:

"A very old man moved from the house next door. It stood vacant for a while, and then I saw new vans, new trucks, and new cars disappearing behind the iron gates. I never saw any furniture moved in, and it was unfurnished. I'd lie on top of my *mirador* and watch the strange goings-on.

"One day I went to the real estate agency and asked, 'Have you rented George's house in La Floresta?'

"She said, 'Yes, to the nicest Mexican family.' They owned avocado groves in some town I'd never heard of. 'Well,' I said, 'they certainly have a strange way of moving in. There's no-body living there and no furniture—only new cars. Probably stolen.' 'Don't tell me we rented to drug dealers,' she said. 'Don't worry, you'll be safe.'

"I didn't feel safe. She said she'd talk to someone, but in ten days, nothing had happened. My gardener talked to the manager of the neighborhood association. They got up on my wall and started writing stuff down in their notebooks. One man jumped off the wall and raised his finger to his lips, indicating I should be quiet.

"The next day, while my friend and I visited, we heard a car door slam. We looked through the living room window and saw six swat team guys coming around the corner, all dressed in gray, with big guns."

I moved to the edge of my chair.

"The head guy said to me, 'Come with us, Señora,' and we went out to my garden. They didn't climb the fence; they jumped it, and positioned themselves all over my wall, on my *mirador*, and in my tree. My friend and I hightailed it into my house. They got one little old guy and ten vehicles. Evidently, they were stealing from dealers and bringing them here. I lived through that, and everything else has been a piece of cake."

Britt got up and slung her purse over her shoulder. "It's been a hoot, but I've gotta scoot. Can't be late for my tennis match."

"Thanks," I said. I walked Britt to the door and watched her get into her sexy yellow convertible, thinking, Nah, not a Q-Tip.

Postscript:

Britt moved to Ensenada about six months later. Her son purchased a mobile home for her so she could be closer to the family. She still enjoys her sunshine and tennis. After a few months of adjustment, Britt is happily relocated.

11 | **Sweating Bullets**

If you have to support yourself, you had bloody well better find some way that is going to be interesting. And you don't do that by sitting around wondering about yourself.
Katharine Hepburn

June met me at the door, one hand restraining the largest white poodle I'd ever seen. If he stood on his hind legs, he could put his paws on my shoulders. I sucked in my breath. "It's okay, he's harmless." She shrugged her shoulders and said apologetically, "Prince likes to jump on people. I'm working hard to break him of that. Come in, come in." She led me to the back patio.

I sucked in my breath again, this time for a different reason. The mammoth garden astounded me. Slate rocks encircled a meandering fishpond, and mature fruit trees of every description hugged the high brick wall. Although I guessed some landscape architect had planned it, her backyard created that illusion of accidental beauty I so love.

June poured us each a glass of water. Short-cropped light blonde hair accentuated her square jaw line. With broad shoulders and slender legs, her body seemed slightly top-heavy, almost military. However, the extra pounds she carried gave the effect of softness, rather than angularity, to her squareness.

When she smiled, her pale green eyes sparkled. Kind eyes, I thought. Gentle eyes.

June looked as though she had dressed for a business meeting. She wore a brown silk pantsuit with a colorful silk scarf around her neck. Prince curled up on a blanket in a corner of the patio as we took seats at the glass-topped table. She looked young, much younger than I, and I envied her peaches-and-cream complexion. "How old are you, June?"

"Forty-four."

"What brought a youngster like you to Mexico?"

She laughed softly. She spoke softly, too, in contrast to her more commanding appearance. "Youngster? I guess it must seem that way here. My health brought me to Mexico." That answer surprised me. For most folks who contemplate moving to Mexico, the quality of healthcare down here is one of their uppermost concerns.

"There's a tree in Austin that I'm deathly allergic to. The disease is called 'cedar fever.' I'm not unusual. There are many people who get very sick when it blooms. I suffered enormously. Over the course of ten years in Austin, I spent $30,000 on allergy medical care. Insurance covered only part of the cost.

"I had searched out one of the top specialists in Austin. Basically, he took me to the cleaners. He prescribed Prednisone for ten years. It allowed me to get up in the morning, go to work, and come home. But it has some very nasty side effects. I gained 100 pounds. The doctor never said anything like 'This isn't working for you' or 'Let's try something else.' "

"Were you married?" I wondered if she'd been going through this alone or with some support.

"For part of that time I was a very fortunate yuppie wife. I had everything I could ask for. I was thirty-five when I obtained my second degree in interior design. My first degree was in journalism. That same year, my husband and I agreed to a divorce. I didn't have a very good reason for asking for the divorce. I think I was just bored. Something was missing in my life."

June sat up straight in her chair, crossing her hands in her lap. "I took a job with an art museum in public relations and stayed there four more years. By then, I was really sick. I knew I had to take my health back into my own hands. I quit my job, sold my house, and went to the Rio Caliente Spa in Guadalajara. I was thirty-nine. My plan was to stay a month and try to flush this medicine out of my system. I was on a vegetarian diet and a low-stress regimen. One of the things Prednisone does with prolonged use is adversely affect your adrenal glands. That's one of the main power sources in your body. I had no energy and needed a lot of rest."

"Did that month restore your system to working order? Did you begin losing a lot of weight?" I could see she wasn't still packing around that hundred pounds. Maybe thirty, but on her large frame, she carried it well.

"My health improved. I hiked every day, but the diet didn't really work for me. I lost some weight, but not a lot. I didn't know what to do next, when 'Ta-da!' Providence intervened." June threw her hands in the air as if she'd just crossed the finish line.

I smiled. "I love the words providence, serendipity, and destiny. You've no idea how many times they pop up in these interviews—and in my own life. Tell me, what happened?"

"The proprietor of the spa asked me to stay and do public relations and marketing for them. I loved the work. I wrote a cookbook and innovated new marketing programs with the help of some talented individuals."

"Did you speak Spanish?"

"I'd taken Spanish in college many years ago, but wasn't a very good student. Because most of our guests were Americans, Canadians, and Europeans, I had very little need for Spanish."

"Did you have to survive on what you earned there?"

"No, it was frosting. I had very few expenses, because they provided housing and meals. After three and a half years, the proprietor and I looked at each other and said, 'It's over, isn't it?' The work was done and it was time for me to move on."

"Then you came to Ajijic? How did you pick this place?"

"While I was at the spa, I had a car, and on my weekends I'd go on discovery trips. I was impressed with the uncommon beauty of the place. But it was the light that really struck me—probably because of my art background. I kept returning for visits. So when the time came for me to leave Rio Caliente, I moved here."

"You didn't consider going back to the States?"

June picked at a fingernail. "I did. I went back to Austin for six months. Friends let me stay in their large home. I marketed myself heavily during that time. I sent out 2,000 resumes. I worked at it day and night. When there was such minimal response, I figured, for whatever reason, I was no longer a marketable commodity."

June slapped her hands on her lap. Prince bounded over and put his dirty paws on her brown slacks. She stroked his head. "Yuck. He's been in the fishpond. Excuse me while I wash my hands."

When she returned, I said, "I'm surprised you didn't receive a better response. You have so many marketable skills." June shrugged her shoulders. "How did you feel, June?"

"Scared. And discouraged. But as it often happens in my life, I needed to be in that place so destiny could take over. The allergy had taken over my body again and I balked at my inability to direct my own course. I had to let go of needing to be in control."

Leaning forward, she gazed directly into my eyes. "I had a series of dreams during that time, and I paid attention to them. One of the recurring images was of me as a Mayan princess. I felt I would flourish if I returned to Mexico. Then," June snapped her fingers, "as fate would have it, I got a call from a Canadian company who wanted me to come to Mexico—on their buck—to purchase *viejitos* for an upcoming convention they were having in Cancun."

"What are *viejitos*? And how did they find out about you?"

June went into the house and returned with a traditional Mexican doll made from newspapers stained with coffee. Not exactly like papier-mâché, the pieces of newspaper are folded into shapes resembling the various body parts and then glued together. "This is a *viejito*—a little old man." I nodded. I'd seem them at most street markets. You could buy them for as little as fifty cents. They were incredible.

June put down a magazine in front of me and opened it up to a picture of her. "Someone at this Canadian company had read this article written for the Canadian airline's magazine about me and the spa. Out of the blue, he called me to ask if I'd be interested." June looked at me and smiled. "The spa tracked me down in Austin. Can you believe the timing?

"While I was in Mexico, I visited Ajijic again and received an offer to work in public relations at one of the larger real estate offices. My life was back on track—or so I thought."

"That's when I met you," I said.

June nodded, then pursed her lips and shook her head. Her jaw tightened and her words whizzed through the air like darts. "It was horrible. I couldn't tolerate working for that man. I felt disrespected. I'd earned my stripes in PR, but all he wanted was a go-fer. We didn't like each other. He fired me. I'd never been fired in my life."

"Why did he fire you—if I might be so bold?"

"Because I told him, in the course of a heated argument, to basically 'fuck off.' It came from somewhere deep within the core of my being. I'd never said that in my life to anyone. Part of me must have known I didn't belong there and it wouldn't be a healthy place for me to work. That subconscious part of me acted upon that knowledge." June breathed deeply and shook her head. Then she laughed, a nervous, staccato laugh. "I would have fired me, too."

"That might have been the best thing that could have happened to you, June—even if you couldn't see it at the time." I hesitated. "Financially, did you need the job?"

"Yes. I had depleted my savings during the six months in Austin and I needed money. I'd tried the job market in the States, so that didn't seem like an alternative. This was the first time in my life I needed to earn a living by doing things on my own."

"I think the last time I saw you, you were putting together some kind of Spanish lessons combined with local travel."

She nodded. "Someone in Texas hired me to develop a Spanish language course for their businessmen. That met with mixed success. Then I was hired by the *Guadalajara Reporter* to write the art column. That wasn't exactly a moneymaker, either."

"What else?"

"A couple hired me to do their daughter's wedding. I had planned a lot of social events when I worked at the museum. One time I orchestrated a wine tasting for 5,000 people. So I knew how to do those things."

"That would be my idea of hell. I could never do something like that." I laughed. "That's what secretaries are for. Even my daughter told me I should have a secretary here in Mexico. I told her I didn't think there was a job description for a secretary to a retired person. I'm a big idea person. I always screw up on the details." June squeezed a lime into her water. No liver spots on her hands yet. "At least now that I'm a senior citizen," I continued, "I can blame my screw-ups on 'senior moments.' "

June sipped her water and sighed, a contented sigh. "By and large, I got by doing these miscellaneous jobs, but there were some months I sweated bullets."

"What are you doing now?"

"I'm writing a how-to book, based on research."

"How to what?"

"How to make a phone call, how to deal with the bank, how to get your shoes repaired. It's a book for people who are either visiting the Lakeside or have recently arrived. One of my strengths is research." She refilled our glasses of water. "For example, in design school, I wrote a grant proposal to NASA to research the most effective colors in the space station. We got the grant. That was a fun project."

"I bet it was. You're going to self-publish your book?"

"Yes. I met someone willing to bankroll the project and ·

I'm writing the book, along with several guest authors. I've got six researchers walking the streets. I'm not trying to sell the area, but rather provide readers with the nuts and bolts of life at the Lakeside. I'm telling readers where they can get their car repaired or find a new battery for their watch or hearing aid."

"I needed that book when I first moved here," I said. "No one told me I had to call and have someone fill up my natural gas tank. Gas had always mysteriously shown up in my house. I'm not a stupid person, but one day I was at a friend's house when the gas truck showed up. I asked, 'What's he doing?' She looked at me like I was from another planet. 'He's filling up the gas tank.'

" 'Do I have to call him to fill up mine?' I asked. She nodded. Duh! I'd been living here for three months. The gas tank was on top of my house, and I didn't know I had to check to see when the needle was in the red zone and call the gas company. Now I do."

June laughed. Telltale laugh lines creased her creamy smooth skin. "We all feel stupid when we first get here. I wanted to know the history of the lake, how the mountain ranges were formed, about our local volcanoes, and what our local flora and fauna are. I couldn't find the information anywhere. That's when I conceptualized this book.

"You can tell how passionate I am about this." She wriggled in her chair like a teenager. "I know that writing and publishing this book is my purpose in life. It's what I'm meant to be doing."

I straightened my back and glared at her with mock indignation. "You can't have that purpose. It's mine!"

We both had a good laugh.

"Let's talk about your life in Mexico now," I said. "Do you feel you've integrated yourself into the local culture?"

"My Spanish came back quickly, it turns out. Although I'm still horrible at grammar, I have a good ear and a good accent. That helps tremendously with communication. Also, my housemate, Charlie, has a special gift."

I was hoping the conversation would get around to Charlie. I knew they had rented a house together shortly after she moved to Ajijic. Charlie was one of the few young, good-looking guys in town. I wanted to know how she had managed that. *Meow.*

"Charlie has always known he would live in Mexico. He loves the culture and has many friends in the Mexican community. He talks to the maids, the kids in the neighborhood, and the people passing by. Because of his outgoing nature, we get invited to a lot of local functions. And when I worked for the paper, I was forced to get out and talk to a lot of people—especially artists. Many were Mexican, which meant I needed to speak Spanish." She put her hand to her heart and took an audible breath. "Artists are special people. They give me an insight into things I would not otherwise have understood.

"Also, I have a dear Mexican friend who is trilingual. She's taught me a lot about the culture and opened many doors for me."

"What's *not* working for you here—your trials and tribulations?"

"I *hate* the drivers." She grimaced. "It seems like there is only one rule and that is 'there are no rules.' And I can't get used to the fact that you aren't able to conduct business with a single phone call. In many instances, it takes three or four calls, and often one or two personal visits. It's so unproductive. And I don't like having to lock up my car. It was broken into right in front of my house."

"That's where I parked my Mazda," I said. "I'd love someone to steal it. The MX is a great little car, but it's not designed for Mexican roads. It's too low to the ground for the *topes* [speed bumps] and potholes. And you can't get parts for it. I'm going to buy my friend's 93 Ford Explorer. That'll be a much better car."

"I came down with a Bronco." June stretched out her legs and crossed her feet. "The mechanic who repaired it screwed up. It exploded and burned. We barely got out with our lives. Now I have a Nissan."

"Jeez, Louise. Did you have any recourse?"

Midlife Mavericks

"The mechanic gave us our money back for the bad job—
if you consider that recourse. I had the car fully insured, but it
took months to get any payment."

"Anything else you can think of that's difficult for you living and working in Mexico?"

June thought a moment before saying quietly, "I have few
peers. That's difficult for me."

"Because you're young and single?"

She nodded, pushing her lower lip up into her upper lip.
"And working. I would love to be dating, but there's no one
available, and I don't see myself dating Mexican men."

"Why not?"

"Because the cultural differences are so great. I've been on
my own for many years, and I'm an independent American
woman. That's the way I'm wired, and there's nothing I can do
to change that. Maybe, if I met a Mexican man who was extremely international and free-minded..."

I couldn't help but ask, "So you and Charlie are just
housemates?"

She laughed. "Charlie is gay. We met when we had both
just arrived. I instantly liked him. He's a very giving and kind
person." She reached over and tapped my hand. "You'll like
this. When I was in Austin, I had my horoscope done. I
learned that I would be living in a foreign country and I would
meet my twin. It was serendipitous that Charlie and I met. Being with him is like being with trusted family. I feel very lucky
about that. Harmony is very important to me."

Like June, I'd lived alone for many years. I couldn't imagine sharing my space with anyone, male or female, straight or
gay, at this time in my life. "What about having your own
space, June?"

"Because we're not in a relationship, there's no problem
with space. We each have our own bedroom. He travels a lot,
and I love that he does."

I glanced through the sliding glass doors into her living
room. She had unique, expensive furniture, clearly not made in
Mexico. "You brought your furniture from Austin?"

June nodded. "I collect furniture. Because I'm an interior designer, furniture is one of my favorite things in the world. I'm glad to have it down here, but I wouldn't recommend my method."

"Which was?"

"I hired a cut-rate mover and some of the furniture was missing altogether. Stolen. Other furniture arrived banged up and broken. Charlie helped when they were unloading. He screamed at them to lift the furniture over the cobblestones rather than dragging it across them. I fixed what I could and learned a hard lesson. You get what you pay for."

I finished off my glass of water and refilled it from June's hand-blown glass pitcher. "Are you covering 'cost of living' in your book?" I asked.

"No. I avoided that. Our target audience is travelers, not residents."

"I think my readers want to know. What does it cost you to live here each month?"

June thought a minute. "About $1250. I eat out whenever I want, sometimes twice a day. I have a full-time maid. She cooks if I plan for it. She'll do anything I ask her to. We have a gardener and someone to walk both our dogs." She smiled broadly. "I don't have to iron my clothes or make up my bed. Those are things I could never find time to do on top of my busy schedule. They are huge luxuries."

Prince wandered over to the fishpond again and June groaned.

"Last question. What lessons have you learned since moving to Mexico?"

She crossed her hands in her lap, studying her thumbs as they encircled one another. Finally, she looked up at me. "After I was fired, when I was freelancing, I worried that I might be committing both financial and professional suicide. But I landed on my feet, working for myself and doing work I am passionate about. I think the lesson here is, do whatever you have to do to get past setbacks. Lose sleep, sweat, cry...and then get up and do what you're supposed to be doing with your life."

I thanked June and hugged her at the door before leaving. Her hair smelled of peaches. As I began the drive home, I thought about the lesson she had learned. Why, I wondered, do so many of us reach middle age before we figure out what the heck we are supposed to be doing with our lives?

Ah well, as they say, "Better late than never."

Postscript:

June published her book in July 2000. It's titled Mexico's Lake Chapala and Ajijic: The Insiders Guide to the Northshore for International Travelers *and can be ordered at the following website: www.chapalaguide.com. When she's not walking on clouds, she's busy marketing. Anyone considering visiting the Lakeside should buy one.*

12 | Rambo's Sister

It took me a long time not to judge myself through someone else's eyes.
Sally Field

I reached toward the top of the gate and yanked a short piece of rope. The cowbell tied to the other end clanged, but to no avail. I was waiting, wondering what to do, when I heard Dakota round the corner, approaching at a trot.

Breathless, she reined in her horse. "Sorry I'm late." Her long brown hair was tied at the nape of her neck in a bright-yellow bandana and her mahogany-brown eyes matched those of her roan mare. I detected a certain guardedness as she gave me a quick once-over, cocked her head, and dismounted. "This is Brava," she said, nuzzling her horse's mane. With high cheekbones and that tall, bones-only frame you see on the cover of *Vogue,* Dakota struck me as both proud and vulnerable.

We entered through two large black iron gates into a scene right out of the Wild West. Brava had claimed the front yard as her corral and stable. The odors of dung and wet hay assaulted me as we headed toward her front door, carefully avoiding piles of manure.

Inside the small house, simple furnishings provided the bare essentials. Fruit crates served as bookcases. Sheeting tacked above the windows tried in vain to keep out the flies. Doors led from the small living/dining room into two diminutive bedrooms.

"Forgive the mess," Dakota said, sucking in her lower lip. "I've been really sick." The front bedroom was stacked window-high with hay. I sneezed and my eyes began to water. "It's the only place I can keep it dry and out of Brava's reach." Dakota shrugged her shoulders with a what-can-a-gal-do expression.

Different strokes, I thought.

Because of my hay allergy, we moved the interview to a local Tex-Mex restaurant. Three Mexican cowboys sat at the bar drinking Coronas. Dakota introduced me to the owners at the only occupied table. We chose a table far in the back, away from curious ears and blaring mariachi music, and ordered nachos and iced tea.

Dakota's shoulders were tense, her laugh loud, and her voice constricted. I guessed her to be in her late forties. "Have you always been a horsewoman?" I asked, trying to ease her discomfort.

"For a very long time. Ever since I moved from California to Oregon. I had five acres there and lots of room for my first horse, Whinny. Unfortunately, there weren't many places I was allowed to ride him. It's wonderful now, keeping Brava close by and riding along the lakeshore or on any street we want."

"You moved to Oregon after you were divorced?"

"Yes. My kids were grown and I was a registered nurse. I've always preferred country to city living. Now it's essential."

"Why now?"

Dakota smoothed her hair back and retied her bandana around a ponytail at the nape of her neck. "Five years ago I had a silent stroke. I didn't find out about it until almost a year and a half later, after the hospital staff had accused me of being loco *en la cabeza*—crazy in the head." She tapped her forehead with her finger and rolled her eyes. "I knew I was making too many mistakes. I forgot important things and I became upset easily. People could look at me cross-eyed and I'd get angry.

Finally I saw a neurologist, who discovered I'd had a stroke. By then I'd lost my job and I had an uphill climb to prove, in retrospect, it was a medical problem. The administration thought it was just sour grapes on my part.

"While I fought with the system over a disability settlement, life was pure hell. Without work, I couldn't keep up my mortgage payments, so I eventually rented out my small home and moved into a deserted school bus on the outskirts of my property. I was freezing and eating in shelters." Dakota bit her upper lip, struggling to hold back tears. My heart went out to her.

"The day before foreclosure, the very day, my property finally sold. I was so fed up with bureaucracy I just wanted to escape, to disappear. I decided to move to northern Washington, where my friend had a small place without running water or electricity." She picked a pepper off her nachos. "It was a stupid idea, but I didn't know what else to do. I was afraid and lonely."

"What about your kids?" I asked, "Couldn't they help?"

"No." I could tell by the abruptness of her answer that the subject was off-limits.

"Anyway," Dakota continued, "two days after the sale was final, I received a letter from my mother. She had moved to Mexico several years before. She told me she was having a biopsy and asked me to visit her. We'd never been close, but I couldn't ignore the timing. I figured my totem was looking out for me, so I went." She fingered the small pouch she wore on a leather thong around her neck and said, "It was love at first sight between me and Mexico. The biopsy turned out okay and I never left."

"How are you feeling now? Have you recovered some of your lost abilities?" I had been watching for stroke symptoms and hadn't seen any. Dakota seemed nervous and high strung, but there was no detectable slurring, sagging, or limitation of movement.

"I'm much better now, but I still struggle with short-term memory and am easily over-stimulated. I'll never nurse or earn big bucks or work eighty-hour weeks again, but here in Chapala"—she studied the nacho in her hand—"I can afford to live simply and even eat out occasionally. This place has all the amenities of modern life, yet it's straight out of a Western movie."

"Perfect for you and Brava?"

She nodded. Dakota focused on her hands as they clasped and unclasped.

"When did you get your horse?"

"After I bought my house in El Chante. Man! Talk about mistakes. I used what was left from the sale of my property in Oregon. Through the help of Manuel's friends (he was my boyfriend at that time), I found this rundown little two-bedroom place far out of town for only $17,000. I poured another $1,300 into it and fixed it up real cute. That's when I bought Brava. The lot next to me was empty and it was perfect for her. I thought my luck had finally changed. I had a home, a Mexican boyfriend, Brava, two cats, and a dog. My disability case had been settled and I expected to start getting monthly payments of $800. Life was pretty fine until..."

Dakota coughed and motioned to the waiter for two refills. *"Dos mas, por favor."* Her Spanish was passable but fluency was a long way off.

After the waiter left, I prompted her. "Life was pretty fine until?"

"The rainy season came. In one large downpour, I watched my living room wall spread apart two inches. The ground underneath was sand, and no matter how many steel bars supported the bricks and cement, when the earth moved, the house moved."

I'd heard other horror stories about building in Mexico and had experienced some of the hassles firsthand. No codes, no inspections, and no lawsuits.

Dakota continued. "I had no other place to live, no more money to invest in the house, and someone had misplaced my claim, so for six months I was living on just $167 a month."

"Jeez, Louise," I muttered. "I can't imagine how Brava could live on that, let alone you and your entire menagerie." I wondered why her mother didn't help, but my intuition told me not to broach that subject.

Head lowered, fingers entwined, Dakota whispered. "It was starvation level and very frightening. We ate a lot of beans, rice, and tortillas. Manuel taught me how to survive. We picked fresh fruit and vegetables and ate like the poorest of Mexicans." Dakota smiled and sank back into her chair as though the worst part of her life was over, as well as the hardest part of our interview. "At least my teeth are whiter!"

In response to my puzzled expression, she explained, "Mexicans have very white teeth. It's because of all the corn they eat.

"When my disability payments started rolling in, Brava and I moved from El Chante to our home here in Chapala—one bedroom for me and one for Brava's hay." As though she had read my mind, she added, "I was supposed to get the lot next door for Brava, but after I paid my first and last, the landlord changed his mind. So my front yard is now her stable."

Dakota laughed, a scratchy, hesitant laugh that might have been recorded off a 33-rpm record. I could detect some uncertainty. "Things aren't like they were in the old days, that's for sure. But I'm really happy here. I'm even happier than I was before my stroke. Sometimes life has a strange way of teaching me lessons. God must have a weird sense of humor." She smiled—a genuine, comfortable smile.

"I still eat at the corner taco stands. It's habit now. I feel guilty spending 100 pesos for dinner. That's almost a third of the weekly wage for a Mexican family, whose average income is only forty-five U.S. dollars."

"What about your health and medical insurance?"

"I don't have any insurance. I'm too young for Medicare in the States, and down here it came down to a choice between my animals and health insurance. The animals won. I'm just recovering from a serious bout with amoebas, and my doctor lets me pay his bills over time. I order my own lab work, and if I see a problem, I take the test results to a doctor."

"As an ex-nurse, Dakota, what do you think about the quality of medical care here?"

"You have to be careful choosing your doctors. One-third of them aren't even licensed. That's from a government study. They went to medical school but never graduated."

Dakota pulled off her bandana and smoothed her hair into it again. "I learned this the hard way. About six months ago, I got into this snarl with a neighborhood yearling that was jealous of Brava. I lost. The horse reared up, broke my arm, knocked me down to the ground, and stomped on my leg. I went to a local clinic where the doctor took X-rays. He said my arm was broken and I had a fractured femur. He put a cast on the arm and splints on my leg and asked me to come back in a few days to see an orthopedic surgeon from Guadalajara. He charged me 1,000 pesos.

"When the swelling went down and I limped into the bathroom on my own, I discovered I could put weight on that leg. Ho! I thought. If this femur was really fractured, I couldn't walk on it.

"What did you do?"

"I was pissed. I went back to the clinic and asked to review the X-rays. I couldn't see any fracture. The duty nurse agreed with me. I took the X-rays into the doctor's office, threw them on his desk, and said, 'I don't think you realize I'm a nurse. Show me where the fracture is.' He stood up, pulled out his wallet, and gave me my money back. It's important to be an informed patient here in Mexico as well as in the States. Some of the doctors are excellent and some are frauds."

"That's true of most things down here, isn't it? I learned the same lesson with my house—you need to be an informed buyer. Lawsuits are unheard of and there are precious few means of recourse."

She laughed and leaned back, stretching her long legs under the table. "Unless you're a rich Mexican. Then you have all kinds of means."

"I don't think that's called 'means,' Dakota. It's called *mordida* or *payola*." We were both laughing. "Forgive me. We were talking about the Mexican medical system."

"I like the fact that herbal remedies are offered side by side with modern medicine. Two doctors I know give free medical care to the poor, and if the patients can't afford medicine, then the doctors tell them what herbs to take.

"You know those women on the corners who are steaming and selling roots?" I nodded. "Those are yams—wild Mexican yams. They're the basis for most of the progesterone treatments in the world and one of the major ingredients in cortisone. Mexican women don't have menopausal symptoms because they eat foods with natural progesterone. I make my own hormone treatment."

"No hot flashes?" She shook her head, and I wished I'd talked with Dakota earlier. Mine weren't as bad as some of my friends', but I'd rather do without them. "Do you really make your own?"

"Mm hmm. I studied herbal medicine for seven years and I'm continually amazed at the roots and herbs available in our street markets. There's generally no need for costly medicines if you know a little about the basics."

"Maybe this will be your next business venture," I suggested. "There are many women lakeside who need hormone replacement therapy, me included." The tenseness was draining out of Dakota's body.

"Do you worry about safety here?" I asked.

"No, not physical safety. About the only crime here is theft, and except for Brava, I don't own anything worth stealing. Why own something if you have to worry about it?" she asked rhetorically.

I thought about my computer, stereo, and camera equipment for a minute. I'd hate for any of those to be stolen; however, I didn't have homeowners insurance or theft insurance. Homes don't burn when they're made of brick and cement. When I checked into theft insurance for my electronics, it was so costly that I decided I could save enough on the premium to replace any stolen goods.

I picked up the last nacho, pulled apart the stringy cheese, and stuffed it into my mouth, mumbling, "Think you'll stay here forever?"

"In Chapala? Probably not. It's getting more crowded, more commercial, and more expensive. There's so much of Mexico I want to explore, but I need to improve my Spanish before I move out of an area where I can get by in English. It's difficult for me to learn with half my right brain destroyed. Manuel taught me some Spanish, so I speak well enough to get by.

"Most Mexicans appreciate our trying to speak Spanish, and the people are so caring and helpful. When my car stalled in front of my house, five young men from the neighborhood offered to help me. When I was sick, the Mexican lady across the street came and cleaned my house and her husband raked Brava's yard.

"I feel protected and safe here." She paused a minute, eyes focused on her hands. "It's kind of a double-edged sword, though," Dakota said, leaning forward over clenched fists. "The neighbors watching over me make me feel safe, and at the same time I feel my privacy is invaded." She lowered her voice. "There are no secrets in Mexican neighborhoods."

"What about you and Manuel? Are you still together?"

"No." Dakota readjusted her bandana again. Her long hair reminded me of burned corn silk. "But I learned some important cultural lessons during that relationship. There were mucho misunderstandings, partly due to language difficulties and partly due to cultural chasms.

"In the traditional Mexican family, women are never alone until they become grandmothers. It's an older brother's job to protect his younger sisters, and when he becomes a boyfriend or husband, he looks after his woman in the same way. I felt suffocated. I couldn't go shopping without Manuel's head on my shoulder." She must have noticed my quizzical look. "He's shorter than me," she explained, holding her flat hand up to the bottom of her nose to indicate where the top of his head came.

"It's really okay," Dakota assured me. "I'm a loner for the

most part. I need to force myself to go out and socialize. It's difficult to find my kind of people here—they live in nooks and crannies or on the outskirts of town. They've integrated into the Mexican communities. For now, though, it's okay. I'm learning to relax and making more time to read and explore with Brava. It's difficult after so many years as a workaholic.

"I'm also understanding the culture better—what's acceptable and what's not." With a wicked glint in her eyes, Dakota said, "They call me *hermana de Rambo*—Rambo's sister. I'm not sure if I should take that as a compliment or not. Manuel's friends gave me that nickname when I started riding Brava. It's not considered ladylike, I was told, to ride astride my horse. Ladies ride sidesaddle.

" 'In your dreams,' I told him."

Dakota folded her hands in front of her. "You know, Chapala isn't unlike a small Midwestern town. Everyone talks, everyone gossips, and everyone knows everyone. Locals say there are only about three or four extended families lakeside. And families are everything. Everything."

She put the heels of her hands on the table, as though she were going to scoot her chair back. "By the time I get all the little cultural subtleties figured out, like not having a man in my home without a chaperone, I'm sure I'll be the subject of conversation at many family dinners." She smiled, and then relaxed back into her chair. "What else do you want to know?"

"Talk to me more about the cultural differences."

"Well, I finally figured out that what we ex-pats think of as a time problem in Mexico is really a priority issue. Family comes first, friends come second, and strangers and customers come last. More important than an appointment is taking your brother to his girlfriend's if his car is broken down. In Mexico, it's customary to stop and talk when seeing people you know. It's considered rude to just wave and walk on by with our American 'Hi, how are ya?' Sometimes that makes them late— . by our standards, not by theirs."

Her observation made me wonder why, considering the lack of concern most Mexicans have about time, watches are hawked on so many street corners. As I pondered that, Dakota continued. "Intercultural relationships are seldom easy. Although it's possible to be accepted as a friend into Mexican families, marrying into one would be a real challenge for liberated women like us."

Liberated? I wondered briefly if I was more liberated because of my pseudo-financial security, or if Dakota was more liberated because she was free of material bonds and expectations, both internal and external. She had sunk to the bottom and risen like cream to the top of the pitcher. Dakota was teaching me lessons on simplicity, survival, and values.

"Tell me, Dakota. Even after your failed relationship with Manuel, a house that came apart at the seams, and your recent bout with amoebas, you still want to live here?"

"Oh yes. I love the freedom...and the sounds of Mexico."

"Explain, please."

"Where else can I keep a horse in the front yard without neighbors complaining to the authorities? And on every street in these Mexican villages, there's a feeling of life—day and night. In the suburbs of Oregon, everyone goes into their own little box at night. If there's a barking dog, the pound comes by. If kids shoot off firecrackers, the police come by. There wouldn't be enough police in all of Mexico to do anything about the fiesta fireworks, even if they wanted to—which they don't. Every festival, from six in the morning to two a.m., kaboom, kaboom! I love it that freedom of expression and individuality are honored here, rather than condemned."

Dakota chewed on the inside of her cheek and wove her fingers together. Finally she said, "These last few years, I've had to make tremendous adjustments. Losing my job and my home in Oregon, along with pieces of my brain, has made me question my own karma. But here in Mexico, I've found the next best thing to living in the Gold Rush days—wide open country, human dignity, a place to forge my own destiny, and a country filled with gentle people who look out for me."

"Not so bad, eh?" I heard the influence of my many Canadian friends creep into my speech.

"Not so bad."

I paid the waiter and we walked back to Dakota's house. In her front yard, she mounted Brava, whispering in the roan's ear and stroking her graying mane. We said our goodbyes and, sitting tall, Dakota headed south toward the local *mercado* for some vittles. I locked the gate behind her and watched the two ride off.

Just before she was out of earshot, Dakota turned back to me and shouted, "This is a wonderful life and it's all about freedom."

13| **From Darkness into Light**

> *Action is the antidote to despair.*
> Joan Baez

"I'm going to try my hand at *chiles en nogada* tonight," Sharon had said on the phone. "Why don't you come over early? We can do the interview first, and then you can serve as my guinea pig."

I'd indulged in *chiles en nogada* only once, at my favorite restaurant in Tonala. The chef had stuffed cooked poblano chilies with a concoction of rice, meat, and fruits, and then slathered them with a walnut cream sauce, topped with pomegranate seeds. My mouth watered at the memory.

About five o'clock I turned off the main road from Chapala to Jocotepec and headed up the hill. "The last street on the left, the first house on the left," Sharon had said. Yikes. This was animal country. Poor country. I wondered if I'd made a wrong turn. Instead of a street, I turned down a tiny dirt road, which would likely become a river in the upcoming rainy season.

As I rounded the corner, a bright yellow-and-blue house contrasted sharply with the drab concrete buildings and brick lean-tos nearby. Cows meandered down the opposite side of the road. I stepped down from my Explorer and maneuvered around a pile of dung. A huge growling dog rushed the wrought-iron gates, warning me the hell out of there. I felt as though my ribs were squeezing the life out of my heart. Somehow I managed to reach the doorbell outside the gate without my knees buckling. My terror of large dogs had not abated since a German shepherd had killed my precious poodle only a year before.

Sharon walked out her front door and, after a quick wrestling match, grabbed the dog's collar. Thin, straight hair, reminiscent of polished mahogany furniture, nicely complemented her bronze, tanned face. A reserved smile greeted me. "Hold on a minute. I'll put Bess in the backyard. She's really quite harmless, but don't tell the neighbors."

As I waited for her to return, I admired her freshly planted flower garden. It surprised me that her home looked so new. She had told me she'd found a "livable" place out of town for $350 a month. I'd expected more of a dump. Obviously, I thought, Sharon understates.

Slightly breathless, she returned to the gate—without the dog—and led me inside.

"Sharon, this isn't the hovel you described. It's charming."

"Well," she demurred, "it's coming along."

Through the windows of the sparsely furnished living room, I noticed a small back courtyard. On the peach-colored wall above her sofa, she had artistically arranged a grouping of framed photographs portraying the colorful people and markets of Mexico. "Did you take these?" I asked. She nodded. "Very nice," I said.

"Thank you. I'm not a professional by any means, but I do enjoy photography. I've shot hundreds of rolls on my travels throughout Mexico."

I handed Sharon a bag of humongous artichokes I'd purchased at Costco along with a bottle of Chilean white wine, and followed her into the kitchen. She laughed as she emptied the plastic bag. "Are these artichokes?" I nodded. "Mind you, I'm from Alberta and in all my forty-five years, I've never once eaten one. The only artichokes I've seen in the market were scrawny little fellows." She put her hands on her hips and tilted her head. "You'll have to cook them, you know."

"Then I guess I'll have to show you how to eat them, too," I said with a laugh. "There's quite an art to it."

"I'm going to need lessons, eh?" I gathered from the tone of Sharon's not quite Canadian, not quite British, accent that she'd been slightly taken aback.

In the kitchen, lime paint and hand-painted Mexican tiles contributed to an unpretentious, country atmosphere. I wondered about the one empty wall without appliances, furniture, or cupboards. I looked around and saw a very small white refrigerator. "No stove?" I asked.

Sharon smiled, a wry crooked smile, pulling her chin in and tilting her head. "It's not a priority for me at this time. After all, I lived in my trailer for six months with only a three-burner unit. Friends have loaned me a microwave and a toaster oven." She chuckled. "I'm getting to be quite creative, you know. I can cook almost anything with those two appliances."

She poured us each a glass of wine and we moved into her living room for the interview, me on a small sofa and Sharon on one of two *equipale* chairs made from pigskin and woven strips of wood. "Oh, I almost forgot." Sharon dashed into the kitchen and returned with small rounds of French bread, a dish of pâté, and an onion/chili/vinaigrette topping. "I tried to copy the appetizers I had at the Ajijic Grill restaurant. I hope they're okay." She set them, along with a few napkins, on a small glass-topped table made of carved and brightly painted wood.

"Scrumptious," I said, devouring two of them. I shifted on the sofa to face her. "How long have you been in Mexico?"

"Almost one year. It really doesn't seem possible."

"And before you moved here?"

"I worked as a secretary for twenty years in an Alberta hospital—the same one my mother delivered me in." Sharon took a deep breath. "Two and a half years ago, I lost my mother. I have no brothers or sisters. I am divorced. No kids.

Last year, for the first time, I realized I could look around and decide what I want to do with my life."

"When you grow up?" I smiled.

"Exactly—if I ever do." She chuckled. "I've always wanted to live someplace else and to travel. It seemed like the opportune time to try something different."

"Can you describe for me the process that led you to Mexico—your internal process?"

"I didn't find life very fulfilling in Canada. Six months of the year I was housebound. I stayed on the couch and got fat. I went to work in the dark and came home in the dark." She thought a minute. "I had friends there, but I had to make an appointment two weeks in advance to meet them for coffee. Plus, I took anti-depressants off and on for five years."

Sharon rubbed the back of her neck. "After Mom died, I thought a change of scenery would improve my attitude and I'd feel more content at home. I scheduled a three-week archeological tour in Mexico. I thoroughly enjoyed the trip, but when I returned, I still felt discontented." Sharon chewed on a fingernail. "It haunted me. I began to think, What if? What if I took a year off and traveled? What if I went back to Mexico? During my tour in March, I saw enough to realize that the lifestyle and values were quite different here.

"In October, I quit my job. I decided I would give myself a year to try and create a better lifestyle." Sharon leaned over to fix herself an appetizer. Her slim-fitting jeans and sleeveless knit shirt showed off a nicely shaped body and firm, tanned arms. I guessed five-foot-five and size eight. She exuded a kind of aloofness. I'm sure her accent had some influence on my perception.

Sharon lit up a cigarette, then pulled a cord on the ceiling fan. "There, I don't think the smoke will bother you with the fan on." She inhaled with some affectation. "The proceeds from selling my mum's house created a small windfall for me. It was free money, in that respect, and I felt I could gamble a little, do what I wanted to."

"You have no monthly income now?"

"Only interest from whatever savings and investments I've made. I still have my own house in Edmonton to sell, but it's heavily mortgaged, so that's not going to net me much."

I nodded. "The bank owned most of mine, too. But the profits enabled me to buy a little house down here. I paid only $48,000 dollars for my house four years ago." Sharon looked up, surprised. "Prices have escalated rapidly in the past four years," I explained. "I've put about $30,000 into it, but I think I could get $150,000 if I sold it."

She blew a pipeline of smoke toward the ceiling. "I wouldn't buy a house, because I'm not sure I'm going to stay here. The Lakeside serves as a great home base because of the network and the English-speaking community; but once I improve on my Spanish, I may move someplace else in Mexico."

A longhaired gray cat crept into the dining room from the back bedroom and curled up at Sharon's feet. "That's Porgy," Sharon said.

"Please fill in the blanks for me, Sharon—from the time you quit your job to when you arrived in Ajijic."

"Winding up here was purely a fortuitous coincidence. My plans were to head south, through the western U.S. and into Mexico. I had no particular destination in mind. I had purchased a van and a seventeen-foot trailer. Mind you, I'd never pulled a trailer in my life. Even now, a year later, I can only drive it forward. I had to leash Bess and harness Porgy whenever they were out of the trailer. They accepted the traveling rather well, though."

"Were you afraid, traveling alone?"

"Terrified is a better word."

"Of what?"

Sharon reminded me of a cat lazing in an armchair, keeping its emotions very much under control. "This vague feeling of paranoia about what might happen, what could happen, stayed with me. I almost lost the whole rig in Oregon when my ball-hitch loosened up." She shivered. "That would have been a quick end to my trip and me, only two weeks into it." Sharon reached across the coffee table for an ashtray, flicked her ashes into it, and then dangled her arm behind her chair, cigarette gripped between her fingers.

"Where did you cross the border?"

"At Mexicali. It took me a while to get up the nerve. I knew once I crossed, I would be in unknown, foreign territory and unable to communicate."

"Had you done any research on driving in Mexico?"

"Yes, quite a bit. I contacted people who either lived in Mexico or had traveled here extensively. I ordered a number of books." She grinned. "That's when I found your column on the Internet. Your story gave me a lot of inspiration."

"I'm glad," I said. "I remember receiving copies of the travel reports you were writing for your hometown paper. I enjoyed seeing Mexico again from your fresh perspective, coupled with that dry sense of humor."

Sharon crossed her legs, leaned back into the chair, and grinned. "I always wanted to write. I think serendipity played a major role. The people I purchased my trailer from wrote a publicity release, and my local Edmonton paper picked it up. They asked if they could send a photographer out." She brushed her hair off one side of her face. "I asked if the paper would be interested in some stories from the road. They said yes."

A broad smile filled her face. "They were handing me my career change on a silver platter. They assigned me six months of articles and purchased my photos as well."

"Did that offer make you think of yourself in a different way? You'd been a secretary for twenty years and all of a sudden you had this writing opportunity."

"Yes, and it added to my terror. When you make such a major change, you lose your definition of self. You don't know where you're going to end up. You just put yourself out there. But somehow, when any crisis arises or any problem happens, someone turns up to help. It never ceases to amaze me." Sharon leaned forward. The pitch of her voice rose slightly and her speech quickened.

"If you do put yourself out there, the information comes,

the assistance comes, you have new friends. You make space in your life for these new things to happen—and they do. I'm not sure how it works, but it does."

"Perhaps," I suggested, "you make space in your life by emptying a part of it?"

"Yes. I agree with that. There's room for new experiences and new people, but it's very scary to let go of the familiar and the safe. And not knowing the language frightened me. I took a couple months of Spanish classes after I quit my job and before I headed south. I had difficulty retaining what I'd learned, because I didn't use it. And it wasn't Mexican Spanish, it was Castilian Spanish."

"With a lithp?"

After she stopped chuckling, Sharon said, "Yeth, with a lithp. The teacher came from Barthelona." She stood up. "I must check on the chilies. Be right back." Sharon disappeared into the kitchen and I helped myself to another hors d'oeuvre. From the little I knew about Sharon, I would never have pictured her taking off into a Third World country by herself without knowing the language.

"When I crossed into Mexicali," Sharon said, licking her finger as she returned to her chair, "strange things happened. Every time I stopped at a red light, people with something to sell leapt out, pushing their faces right through the open car window. People on bikes crossed the street willy-nilly, and dogs ran in front of the van. It felt like total anarchy. Accurate signs were as nonexistent as dinosaurs."

"In three or four hours, by the time I had reached the RV park in Tecate, I was ready to quit. I pulled into the KOA and asked the fellow, '*Habla inglés?*' [Do you speak English?] He said, '*Muy poquito*' [Very little]. Then he asked me, in perfect Oxford English, 'Do you speak Spanish?' I looked at him dumbfounded. I couldn't shift gears that fast. Then I cracked up and he started to laugh with me. He, along with his son and daughter-in-law, was so helpful. That's been my experience all the way along."

"You were stressed, frightened, and wondering what the

hell you were doing as you crossed the border. Did those feelings accompany you all the way through Mexico or did you
relax as you continued?"

"To a degree it's been with me always and still is, because
I've made such a radical change and I don't know where I'm
going. I know where I'm pausing, but that's a comma in my life
rather than a period." Sharon rested an elbow on the arm of
the chair and leaned her cheek against her open palm.

I liked her analogy, but I didn't think I'd want a period in
my life until my last breath. For me, part of the fun of living is
not knowing what's in store for me around the next corner, or
through the next door. Maybe I could live with an occasional
semicolon.

Sharon continued. "Driving through Baja intimidated me.
Different experiences on the way, like running out of gas, un-
nerved me."

"Tell me."

"I saw a sign that said, "Pemex—30 kilometers." I figured
I could make it that far, but when I got there, the Pemex had
obviously been defunct for years. Cobwebs covered the
pumps. I continued south. When I realized I wouldn't make it
to the next town, I pulled into a ranch. Someone had propped
a rusty old car door on the side of the access road with *"gaso-
lina"* hand painted across it. I pulled up and eight big burly
Mexican men approached my rig."

"Was your adrenaline pumping?"

"Not really. I assumed it would be all right, but I was uncomfortable about the language thing. In my pidgin Spanish, I
managed to communicate my problem. They were more than
accommodating. They scooped a canister of gas out of a barrel
and poured it into my tank. I made it as far as Todos Santos,
where I stopped for six weeks to indulge in a minor nervous
breakdown."

"Why?" This revelation surprised me.

Sharon placed her cigarette in the ashtray and leaned back,
folding her hands in her lap. "I struggled with the 'what have I
done to my life' question. I walked on the beach and swam in

the river, but I simply could not move on."

"Were you taking medicine?"

"No. I'd not taken an antidepressant since I left home. It wasn't a depression, really, so much as a panic attack. I didn't think about going home, I just couldn't move on. I'd sit and chant, 'I'm not ready. I'm not ready.' She smiled. "With no one else in the RV park, only my fur balls heard me."

"What made you finally move on?"

"The heat. I couldn't tolerate the heat. I sweated buckets. I had planned the trip backwards. Baja is not the place to be in the summer. But I'd always wanted to see Baja, and I did." She folded one slim leg underneath herself on the chair. "You know, throughout the trip I felt, in a sense, guided. I needed to make this trip to keep myself alive." In response to my head-jerk reaction, she said, "That sounds dramatic, I know, but I was choking at home. It just wasn't a life I wanted to continue living.

"Then, almost miraculously, at certain points along the way, if I didn't know what to do, someone or something would always turn up to help me along my journey."

"Can you give me another example?"

"In Mazatlan, after they finally released my animals and my vehicles from the ferry, I couldn't find a trailer park. Then I couldn't find anyone who spoke English to help me find the trailer park. Finally, a young lady came by, saw me struggling in sign language with a bellboy, and said, 'I speak a little English. Can I help?'

"Next thing you know, she had five guys involved in the conversation. They called in a couple of police officers. Finally, a jewelry salesman said, 'It's about six blocks. I'll walk you there.' He did. Then he walked me back. I bought a piece of jewelry from him, and he told me all about his girlfriend. The helpfulness of those Mexicans really touched me."

"And how did you end up in Ajijic?"

"I met Janet and Herb and their two daughters in Mazatlan. They were heading for Ajijic. They told me how much they had enjoyed it on a previous trip and invited me to stop by if I got down that way. I didn't plan to stay in Mazatlan long. Just brushing my teeth caused sweat to run down my forehead. I needed to get out of there.

"Another couple and a single guy told me they were caravanning to the Copper Canyon and asked if I'd like to join them. What a wonderful opportunity, I thought. The next day's drive challenged all of us. Locals call that road The Devil's Backbone. The scenery, when I dared take my eyes off the hairpin curves, made me catch my breath. It would have been a great trip for a motorcycle, but not for a van with a 17-foot trailer."

"Then you headed south, toward Ajijic?"

"Yes. I got here in September. The lush green mountains and wildflowers pulled at my heartstrings. The time had come for me to rest. I pulled into the PAL trailer park and joined up again with Janet and Herb. The park is lovely and clean, with a gorgeous swimming pool. After my long solo journey, this was just what the doctor ordered."

We both turned at a shrill whistling noise coming from outside. "The rain birds," I said. "Do you know about them?"

Sharon shook her head.

"They start singing right before the first rain with this unmistakable shrill. They're not really birds, but rather cricketlike creatures, which create that sound by rubbing their legs together. They're called *chicharras*. I hope they're right. I'm ready for cooler and greener and wetter."

"Yes. I'm looking forward to being here this rainy season. I arrived just at the end of it last fall. Let me refill our glasses and check on my culinary efforts in the kitchen. You can probably start your artichokes now. Microwave, you said?" I nodded and followed her into the kitchen. "I want to see how you cook them."

"Easy." I demonstrated. "Cut off the stems and about half an inch off the top. Put some water, lemon juice and chopped garlic in the bottom of the dish, turn the artichokes upside down into the liquid, and then cover them with plastic wrap. These are huge, so maybe twenty-five minutes. When you can easily pull one of the leaves out, they're done." I turned on the microwave, leaned against the sink, and said, "I met you shortly after you arrived. I remember you saying, 'I like this place. I think I might stay here awhile.' "

She nodded. "I'd been gone six months at that time. Originally, I planned on going as far as Chiapas and then returning to Canada. I rented out my house in Edmonton, so I hadn't burned all my bridges." Sharon shrugged her shoulders and smiled. "Somehow I stayed right here on Lake Chapala. The people in the trailer park were about my age and doing similar things in their lives."

"Then about three months ago, you left the park and moved here to Jocotepec. Why?"

"It's a little remote, a half-hour's drive from Ajijic, but as the snowbirds started arriving, the park felt a bit too 'gringoized,' a bit too crowded, and a bit too social. I wanted to live in a Mexican community and work on my Spanish. Here I have room for visitors and a yard for the animals— all for less than I was paying at the park."

"Do you feel safe here? A young, attractive, single gringa?"

"Yes. Bess is a big dog. She sounds fiercer than she is. And the neighbors are friendly. I feel they keep an eye on me, and the goings-on at my house." A wicked little grin crept across her face. "My social life is better than it's ever been. If I'd had this kind of life in Canada, I'd never have left."

I remembered my interview with Angie and how good her social life was here in Mexico; and then Chaz, and how she was struggling to find where she fit in. I thought, Perhaps it isn't so much where a woman lives, but rather her attitude, which influences how good her social life will be.

"What kinds of activities are you involved in?"

"I play volleyball, go dancing, travel, cook, go to parties, and decorate my house. And of course there's my photography and writing."

"You've lost a lot of weight since you came. You look great."

"It's not at all intentional. I'm just more active, more in-

terested. I don't have enough time for everything I want to do.
I need to start looking at job possibilities, because I'm not in-
dependently wealthy. I've met a lot of folks just winging it here,
because they love the lifestyle—not because they're rich and
retired.

"Really," Sharon put some walnuts in the food processor
and turned to me. "What are the alternatives? I can tighten my
belt and live here with less or go back home and get a job. The
latter is most definitely not an alternative for me."

"Final question, Sharon, and then we can eat. How has
this trip changed you?"

She didn't hesitate. "I feel more self-confident. I did it. I'm
more secure with my own resources. I feel more alive, more
gratified about my life these days. It's a beautiful place. I have
new friends. I'm never bored. It's just an entirely different
mindset that I have here in Mexico. The weather makes all the
difference. I don't need Prozac anymore. That six months of
cold and dark can't reach me down here."

A light sprinkle of rain pattered against the kitchen window. "Those rain birds have it right, don't they?" Sharon said.
"I think, perhaps, they do a better job predicting the weather
than your American groundhogs do."

Part III:

Indiana "Joans"

Born too late to ride westward in covered wagons, these midlife mavericks lust for adventure. They long to experience a new culture, to establish roots in foreign soil, to free themselves of society-imposed roles, and to test their own mettle. These intrepid women hark to the call of the unknown and heed the counsel of Yoda in Star Wars: "Try? Try? There is no try. Only do or not do."

14 | The Sky Is Falling!

Love is not all: it is not meat nor drink nor
slumber nor a roof against the rain.
Edna St. Vincent Millay

It was dusk when I pressed the bell, located at tiptoe height on a brick wall smothered with burgundy bougainvillea. The gardener escorted me into Halsie's magnificent Mexican hacienda. I felt as though I'd been transported from Mexico into a gracious New England home. The juxtaposition of her tapestry-upholstered wingback chair and the background of Mexican-style brick archways shouldn't have worked, but it did.

A captivating bronze sculpture of a mermaid, placed off-center on the rosewood coffee table, complemented her mahogany-framed paintings of New England and the sea.

Halsie swaggered in, short-cropped silver hair and deep facial lines proudly proclaiming her seventy-one years. She was fit, with an almost athletic build. Her cotton T-shirt made no attempt to camouflage a double mastectomy.

"I don't give a hoot for prostheses or pretensions," she said, poking her thumbs at her chest. "I'm like Popeye. What you sees is what you gets." She smiled a sage old smile and winked, I think, at my discomfort.

"We'll have some wine on the veranda while we watch the

sunset. It's not to be missed." Without waiting for a reply, Halsie disappeared into the kitchen and returned with a carafe of wine and elegant crystal goblets on an old English silver platter. We sat on wrought-iron chairs at a small Mexican leather-topped table. Birds chirped as water gurgled from a three-tier concrete fountain in the center of her courtyard. She poured us each a glass of wine.

Halsie was right about the sunset. The skies looked like strawberry jam and orange sherbet streaked across a gray flannel tablecloth. I raised my glass. "To your life, Halsie."

As she smiled, her crooked face lit up. I knew she'd been slugged in the face by a mental patient while working at a military hospital years ago. Her nose didn't line up exactly straight, and her disability payments didn't begin to compensate her for the continual pain she had with her jaws and teeth.

"My life?" Halsie smiled. "I've helped lots of souls into this world—369 babies, including four of my own. That's made my life pretty wonderful and worthwhile. I've got six grand children and two great-grandchildren. If the medical profession hadn't started putting so much legal pressure on us midwives, I guess I'd still be delivering babies.

"Well," she sighed, "that part of my life is over and this one's just beginning."

"It's this one I want to hear about, Halsie."

She stood up, hands on hips, jutting out her angular chin. "This is my dream house, my Spanish hacienda. I've been designing it in my mind, brick by brick, window by window, for many years. I could never afford to build it in Southern California, so it remained a dream until three years ago, when I decided to retire in Mexico."

"Some of this stuff I already know about you, Halsie, but I want to get it on tape. You're widowed?"

"No. Divorced. I've been married three times—most of my life. But no more. This dance is mine."

"How did your children feel about your decision?"

"Man, were they outraged when I told them I was moving to Mexico. They worried about my health and safety. My son-in-law, Carlos, grew up in Monterrey, and his horrible childhood experiences in Mexico blinded him to any possibility I could be happy here. They worried how they'd take care of me if anything happened." She tried to laugh, but it came out as a snort.

"You snort just like my mother." We both laughed. The expression "salt of the earth" must have been invented to describe this lady.

"So you just packed up and headed south?" I was amazed at her moxie.

"Not exactly. I arranged to housesit for a friend in Ajijic while I looked around. I bought this small piece of land a few miles out of town and got a quote for building my dream home. I only had enough money for half the house. By then my hacienda was no longer a dream, it was a burning passion." Halsie surveyed her garden with pride. "I just couldn't let go of it."

"I borrowed money from my kids and my friends to pull it off. I was leveraged up to my kazoo, and I was scared to death I'd die before I paid them back." She shivered. "I've never owed money in my life. Being in debt scared me more than the move."

She sat back down and leaned across the table, wine glass in hand. "I bought open land. My friend—the one whose house I was staying in—is the Realtor who sold it to me, so I didn't worry about the deal. Ha!" Halsie threw her head back. "I guess she forgot to mention I'd have to put in my own electric and telephone poles, lay my own cable, and redo the roof. And water... Well, I'll get to that later.

"So my *friend* recommended this contractor. She must have received a kickback. There couldn't be any other reason, because he turned out to be the worst contractor lakeside. Ask anyone. Ha!" She slapped her knee. "That's what we both should've done before we hired him—got references."

I nodded. Halsie and I had first met when she and I were both heavily involved in the construction of our homes. Unfortunately, the same real estate agency referred us both to the same contractor. It was still a sore subject with me, although I was trying to let it go. There were too many beautiful things and beautiful people in Mexico to carry around bad feelings about one or two rotten eggs. We all have lessons to learn when we move to another culture, and this was a lesson Halsie and I shared.

"I've remodeled houses and added on extensions with my own hands," she said. "I have a garage full of electric tools most carpenters would envy. I thought I was a pretty smart cookie. But what I didn't know about Mexican construction nearly killed me—literally. Wherever that bastard could cut corners and save money, he did. I was out there every day. I made sure they followed my plans, but I couldn't judge the quality of the work. I was used to wood framing and wallboard, not bricks and cement—if you could call that mixture of dirt and lime they use cement."

Halsie was a gracious hostess and refilled our glasses as the last of the sun's rays disappeared behind the mountains. She was a contradiction—mermaids and tools, snorts and silver platters.

"This is so beautiful, Halsie. Do you get these sunsets often?"

"Yep, most of the time. And the weather is perfect here. If I just didn't have to put up with these pesky *bobos* in the rainy season, I'd call this place Camelot. I think they're worse down here by the lake. They just swarm around and you can breathe them into your mouth or nose if you're not careful.

"Okay, where was I? Ah. My furniture arrived about a month before the house was finished. I hadn't learned yet about the *mañana* factor in Mexican schedules. My stomach turned, seeing my beautiful antique pieces huddled together in the middle of the rooms, covered with tarps and blankets, while workmen painted around them. It cost me $7,000 to get this stuff here, but I brought it all—except for my fourteen-foot ladder, and I regret that.

"I've had my furniture, china, and crystal since my first marriage, and in my mind's eye, each piece had its prearranged place in this hacienda.

"Finally, they finished. Boy, was it beautiful! From the outside it was picture perfect. The windows were put in backwards, and inch-high cockroaches could crawl on their hind legs through spaces under the doors. There were no shelves in the cabinets or linen closets. My contractor didn't consider those things problems, at least not his problems.

" '*Mas dinero, mas dinero.*' He always needed more money for this, more money for that. I was almost broke when the first rainstorm thundered overhead.

"Upstairs, in my bedroom, the east wall resembled Niagara Falls. I couldn't mop it up as fast as it came down. The wind whipped more rain under the doors and around the windows. Every towel I owned was in service sopping up the water. Images from *Fantasia* and Mickey with those mops and buckets and all that water kept going through my mind. This was a brand-new house with a brand-new roof. Water shouldn't have leaked in, let alone gushed."

Halsie leaned back in her chair and sighed. "My dream house was turning into a nightmare, a soaking-wet nightmare. I couldn't tell my kids. My Realtor friend sided with the contractor. I didn't know where to turn or what to do."

Halsie stared at the wine she was swirling in her goblet. She took a deep breath and continued.

"He came and fixed the roof the next day. The next rainstorm, his fix failed. I was up most of the night swabbing the floor again."

There was something, some strength about Halsie that reminded me of Katharine Hepburn—a kind of doggedness.

"The following morning, I climbed on the roof myself. The damn thing was made of sheetrock, covered with tarpaper, and then topped with those curved terra-cotta tiles that look so beautiful. Rats had torn apart the tarpaper and the sheetrock was soaked. They should've used cement and bricks on the roof, but they constructed the roof when I was away.

"Within a month, my dining room ceiling started to cave in. I moved my teak table into the living room and propped up the ceiling with pieces of pipe. I did what I should have done the first time. I asked around and found a reputable contractor who gave me a quote of $10,000.

"I swallowed my pride and called my daughter to ask for another loan. She said, 'Come home, Mom. It's too much for you to handle down there.' " Halsie pursed her lips and sank back into her chair. "I was beginning to think she was right.

"When the dining room roof caved in, so did I. My nerves were shot and I'd lost my will to fight. He had me licked. An old *gringa* trying to build a house in a macho country is at too big a disadvantage. It was very painful. I made the mistake of paying up front for what I wanted. The money disappeared and I didn't get what I paid for. I had a contractor who put my house together with spit and glue. His attitude was 'If it looks good, then don't complain, lady, you got what you wanted.' "

Halsie took a deep breath and let it out slowly. "Then I had a mild stroke. The doctor told me, 'No more stress.' My daughter lent me the money, and I stayed with her in California while my new roof was installed. I recovered, but I'm not sure all my brain cells have returned to their assigned slots."

"Sounds like that stroke was a wake-up call. Did you follow the doctor's orders and eliminate stress?"

"I tried. My house was supposed to cost $58,000. I paid that crook $63,000 by the time it was finished. Repaired, replaced, and restructured, it cost me another $14,000 and I'm deeper in debt."

Halsie lowered her head and looked at me through her thinning eyelashes. "I know, you're thinking the house will belong to my daughter when I die, but it was very hard to ask her to bail me out when I never should've gotten myself into this situation. I felt like I'd failed and created a financial burden for her. One of my loans is paid now and I can take a financial breather; so, yes, the stress is *mucho* reduced."

"No, Halsie, I was thinking that you've got $78,000 in this house. Surely it could sell for almost twice that. So at least you'll be compensated for your hardships. I looked at building my house as an investment, but you've obviously got your heart and soul wrapped up in this place."

She put both goblets on the tray and shoved her chair back. "It's cooling off. I just baked chocolate-chip cookies, so we'll go inside and have some." She scrambled toward the kitchen before I could object. I wondered if I'd have that much · moxie when I was seventy-one. Halsie set the cookies and two cups of coffee on the dining room table.

"Well," I said, admiring the hand-painted Mexican tiles in her kitchen, "the house looks great now. Are you happy with it?"

She looked a little sheepish. "I'm embarrassed to admit it, but as soon as the roof, water damages, and structural repairs were completed, I decided enough was enough. The contractor had won. I put the house on the market, hoping to get $140,000. The profits would get me out of debt and I'd consider the rest a persecution payment."

The cookies were still warm. I took a bite of one. It was soft on the inside and crispy on the outside. "Delicious. Thank you, Halsie." After a few more bites, I said, "You obviously didn't sell the house."

"My friends talked me out of it. 'The worst is over,' they said. 'Stay and enjoy your dream house.' They were right. As time passed, things became easier. I'm a survivor and I love my home, my friends, and the weather. My daughter would like me to come back to California, but I feel good here. So here I stay. Each day it gets easier. Communication is still a problem, though. Because of my limited Spanish, little things sometimes turn into big things."

"Can you give me an example?"

She snorted. "Yesterday. That's a good example. I asked my gardener to move a bench into my back patio. Later, I looked outside and he was digging up a tree. I really thought he understood and so did he. We both laughed. That was a little thing."

Halsie thought a minute. "Here's a big thing—the water story I promised to tell you. My contractor threatened to cut my water off. He owns the only well in the area. Mind you, it's not registered, so he can't legally sell water from the well. He put tree branches over it and built a fence in front of it so the water company couldn't find it.

"He wanted me to pay for a year in arrears because his workmen used his water to build my house. My Scottish stubbornness surfaced. The cost of water should have been included in the construction cost. Then, on top of that, he wanted me to pay double the going rate, starting from the day I moved in. They don't have water meters here. Costs are calculated per square meter of land, and I had done my research.

"We were at an impasse. My friend had told me to hold out, to threaten him with exposing his illegal well. She thinks I'm such a tough broad, but I have less strength for fighting battles than I used to."

I imagined Halsie had a fair share of tiger left in her tank.

"That week, we had a meeting—him and his wife, me and my interpreter. His wife said to me, 'You paying for water!'

"I said, 'Tell me how much was used and I'll pay you.' "

"She said, 'You pay or no water.'

"I was up the creek. I needed water. My purchase agreement included nothing about water rights, thanks to my *friend* the Realtor. His wife screamed at me, wagging her finger in my face, 'You bad.'

"I could hardly breathe. My pulse was racing. 'Stay calm,' a close friend had coached me. 'Just find out what his bottom line is.' I don't think with my head in situations like this, I react with my emotions. Next thing I knew, I was standing up face to face and wagging my finger in front of her nose. 'No, you bad.' I felt lightheaded and sat down to keep from fainting.

"Finally, as preplanned with my interpreter, I agreed to pay his exorbitant rates if he gave me a receipt with the registration number of his well on it. He blanched. They spoke rapidly in Spanish. The interpreter nodded at me. We ended up with a compromise. The contractor waived all water payments prior to the date I moved in and reduced my monthly rate by half. He gave me a contract for future water and a receipt. It had no registration number on it."

Halsie pretended she had a cigar in her mouth and flashed her eyebrows at me, Groucho Marx style, obviously proud of herself. "Not bad, eh? I always think if I'd been a business-woman like you instead of a midwife, I could probably have handled these problems better—at least with less stress."

Thinking back to my own remodeling experience, I wasn't so sure. I had moved into my Mexican home two months after construction was scheduled to be finished. Completed were the guest bedroom and bathroom; installed were the electricity, plumbing, and a front door. I owned one mattress, two bar stools, and a refrigerator.

Workmen swarmed around me from morning to night, Monday through Saturday. I wore a white paper mask to filter out the cement dust. On the seventh day, in the quiet and calm, I rested. Sometimes I cried; sometimes I marveled at the miracles accomplished the preceding week.

Finally, it was done. But the gas company wouldn't fill my rooftop tank because it had been installed too close to the chimney and might explode. The water heater caught fire because no ventilation had been provided for it. The light fixtures in the house soon burned out because there was insufficient air space around the wires. My Bose stereo stopped working because instead of running the cables inside the walls with the electrical lines, the workmen had strung them, unprotected, across my roof, where the sun and rain destroyed them.

When the phone doesn't work, the water runs out, or lightning zaps the electricity, whom do you call? Where do you go for help? Things seemed so difficult at first, but when I let go, adopting the Mexican attitude of 'It may not get fixed to-day, but it will get fixed,' then life became much simpler.

"No, Halsie, I don't think being a businesswoman would have made any difference. My belief is that what makes life eas-ier here is our giving up control and realizing we have plenty of time for all of life's little surprises. I think we all learn to cope differently. Maybe we need to change our expectations rather than trying to change the reality. Maybe adequacy is okay and excellence is unattainable. Don't you find yourself reordering priorities and letting go of the small annoyances?"

"You have to. Ha! You couldn't survive here if you let all the small things get to you. There's only enough of me left to worry about the big things." Halsie slapped her flat chest and I understood that for her, a big thing was cancer. "Finally," she said, "after all my house disasters, I have some free time to enjoy. I'm sculpting and painting again, decorating, and doing some entertaining. I sculpted that bronze mermaid on the coffee table."

"No! Halsie, she's gallery quality. It's absolutely fantastic." I looked around the dining room. "And that young boy?" She nodded, an embarrassed, yet pleased, grin creeping across her face. "I am truly amazed and in awe. What else do you do?"

"I bought a set of miniature tools so I could make furniture for my dollhouse, and of course there's that pewter soldier collection I painted myself." She waved her hand toward the antique desk, atop which the miniatures stood ready to battle.

A woman of many talents, contradictions, and surprises, I thought. "If you had it to do over, would you?"

She took a minute before answering, curling her lower lip around the upper one. "No, not this way. I was far too trusting and got myself in way over my head—emotionally, physically, and financially. But I'd move here again in a heartbeat.

"My belief is you go for it and iron out the wrinkles as they appear." She lowered her voice and put her hand on her heart. "Sometimes the wrinkles are permanent. Dealing with betrayal and losing a friend over money was hard for me. I guess I'm just a crusty old pie shell with whipped-cream insides.

"Bother, I sound like a sentimental old fool. If I weren't so mulish, I'd be back in California now. But this old lady's got it made." Halsie walked to the front door and turned around. "I have my dream house. My garden is magnificent. The higher altitude has improved my health. My roof no longer leaks. My retirement and disability dollars go a hell of a lot further here than in California. I've made wonderful friends. And I've got some interesting new neighbors."

She motioned for me to join her outside. "Hear that?" she asked, cupping her hand around her ear. It sounded like a fox had sneaked into the chicken coop. "Twenty-six roosters just moved in next door. The guy who rents that property imported them from Oregon and says he's training them for the Mexican Olympic cockfights."

I shook my head. Being such a light sleeper, I was certain I'd have poisoned them by now.

Not Halsie. "Maybe," she said, with a you-gotta-love-em grin, "he'll give me free admission tickets."

Postscript:

After putting her house on the market twice more, she finally sold it. Halsie returned to Southern California to live closer to her family. She rented an apartment two blocks from where she had previously lived and pays $1800 a month rent. She has very little money left for social events and traveling. I asked her, "Why?"

She responded, "Because life is too hard in Mexico." I thought to myself, Hard? For me, it's the easiest my life has ever been. A maid, a gardener, beautiful weather and the time to do whatever I want.

Halsie now enjoys increased peace of mind and her life is much less stressful.

15 | The Fake ID

A teacher affects eternity; he can never tell where his influence stops.
Henry Brooks Adams

Virginia poured us both a glass of water. "I'm fasting," she explained. "I do this once a month to clean out my system. Only water today." She pulled her chair to the table, sat erect with her hands in her lap, and said, "As I was preparing for this interview, it occurred to me there were three important turning points in my life: a jealous husband, a fake ID, and a recession in Japan." She grinned mischievously.

"Okay, Virginia, you've pushed my curiosity button. Now please fill in the blanks." I was surprised at how she'd immediately taken over the interview. Somehow I expected an 81-year-old woman to be less assertive.

The sun trickled through starchy white lace curtains, teasing the freshly painted white walls and daffodil-yellow kitchen cabinets. We sat at a small chrome kitchen table, which reminded me of the one my mom had in the fifties. Virginia's thick black hair was streaked with gray. I chuckled to myself. Built of sturdy stock, with a jutting jaw, she could easily have been Jay Leno's mother.

"I was a WAC in World War II," she began. "When it ended, the Army discharged me and I married Harold. Twenty-three years later, when the boys were off to college, I left him because of his jealousy. I felt like I was living in a straitjacket. When I couldn't take it anymore, I left him and moved to Sacramento, California.

"I'd never worked a day in my life when I was married. After the divorce, I became a medical transcriber, and then I worked three years as a bookkeeper in a Presbyterian Church, eventually ending up employed by a large aerospace company. When they downsized in 1990, I took an early retirement at age seventy-three."

"Wait a minute," I said. "How can you take early retirement at seventy-three?"

She smiled. "They thought I was ten years younger. My neighbor had doctored up my driver's license with his old Underwood typewriter when they hired me. I was really sixty-three. They never would have hired me if they had known. Sneaky, huh?" Virginia tilted her head and raised one eyebrow.

"I enrolled at Sacramento State College and earned a certificate to teach English as a second language. When I finished the two-year program, I rented out my condo in California and flew to Japan, ESL certificate in hand. I had visited there in 1973 and loved it." She sighed. "Unfortunately, my timing was off. With the recession in high gear, there were so many unemployed teachers with experience. Clearly, they weren't going to hire me, a 75-year-old inexperienced woman."

"Were you terribly disappointed?"

She nodded. "Yes, quite disappointed. I returned to Sacramento, still with this overwhelming urge to experience another culture."

Virginia cocked her head, held a finger to her lips, and sat quietly until the church bells finished before she continued. "I had some friends who lived in Ajijic, so I wrote them, asking if volunteers were needed there. They responded right away, saying, 'Come on down.' That was five years ago. They took me many places, introduced me to a few very nice people, and I loved what I saw.

"I told them, 'I'm going home to get my things and I'll be

back.' I had rented my condo in anticipation of moving to Japan and was living temporarily with a friend, so it didn't take me long to get packed up and drive down from California."

"You drove to Mexico by yourself?"

"Sure, why not? My friends suggested this condo development because they thought I'd feel comfortable here. Knowing myself, I agreed. I'm a loner and might never have met anyone if I lived in a separate house. I don't get lonely, but sometimes I get bored. If I go out to the pool or the spa, I can always find someone to talk to when I feel like being social.

"I'm so glad I didn't get a job in Japan. The cost of living is too high there. I would have had to work fifty hours a week just to eat and pay rent." She nodded briskly with one of those Stan Laurel looks on her face. "The Lord knew what he was doing when he put me here where I could do his good deeds."

"You don't need to work in Mexico to eat and pay rent?"

"No. I live comfortably here on $1,200 to $1,500 including my rent. Things are getting more expensive, though. This condo costs $350 per month. My food bill has doubled in the last two years, and restaurant prices have soared. I don't know how people make it here on only $800. Of course I have a car and they might not have those expenses. If they learn to enjoy Mexican food, they can eat cheaply when they go out."

She took a sip of water, leaned forward, and whispered conspiratorially, "So now you know about the jealous husband, my fake ID, and the recession in Japan." The laugh lines around her clear brown eyes hinted at a jovial personality, which contrasted with Virginia's more staid body language. "What else do you want to know?"

"I'd like to hear about your life in Mexico. How do you keep busy?"

"I'm using my ESL training here. A friend introduced me to my first student. She brought a young boy over who had been out of high school for a year because the doctor had told him his eyes were bad. I taught him and his older brother twice a week. Now he's a math major at a local university on a scholarship from The Little Chapel, and I contribute some money every month to help him out.

"Gradually, by word of mouth, I acquired more students. I enjoy teaching the Mexican people. They're so friendly and helpful. I'm down to three students now, which is better for me because it gives me time to pursue other activities I'm interested in, like theater and Spanish lessons."

"You act at the Lakeside Little Theater?" I was impressed.

"No, I don't act. A few years ago I took a course on lighting, and I've worked for the last three winters doing either light or sound for the local theater. I'm anxious to get trained on the new lighting board. The president of the theater stopped me on the street the other day and said, 'Virginia, I hope you'll work for us again this year.' That pleased me.

"I started taking on too many things and had to pull out of some plays. I'm being more careful now with my commitments. This year I did only two plays and worked on the Christmas Cantata."

I remembered last year's cantata. The celestial music, coming from deep within the singers, was as good as any I'd heard in the States.

"And," Virginia continued, "I participate in more cultural events right here in Ajijic than I ever did in California. That's because I hated hassling with the Sacramento traffic and parking. After my first year here, they made me elder of a nearby church, and the following year, senior elder, which meant I was chairwoman of the board and I had an awful lot of responsibilities. I took it very seriously. When I finally resigned that position, I volunteered to take care of the flowerbeds. I still do that. The gardener trims and mows and waters, but he doesn't know how to properly care for the flowerbeds."

"Virginia, you've been here five years now. Can you speak Spanish?"

"When I had nine students to teach, I couldn't find time to study Spanish and prepare for my students' lessons. So no, I don't speak the language. Occasionally, I'll go into a business where no one speaks English, and when that happens, I'm disgusted with myself and I apologize because I cannot speak their language. I'm a guest in their country. They shouldn't have to speak English to me." Virginia leaned closer to me and said with a hint of pride, "Now that I have only three students, I plan to go back to the Spanish Language School in Guadalajara. I'm going to turn down new students until I learn to speak *español.*"

"I attended that same school. It's wonderful, isn't it? The three women who own it have been teaching there for over thirty years, and they know how to do it right." I remembered fondly the Mexican family who had opened their home to me for a month while I studied Spanish in Guadalajara.

Pulling my thoughts back to the present, I asked Virginia, "What else do you do with your time?"

"In my alone time, I like to read and walk." She pointed to a small TV in the corner of the room. "I'd much rather pick up a good book than watch that darn television. Of course, TV would probably help me with my Spanish." Virginia refilled her glass of water and squeezed a lime into it. "What else? I walk at least an hour every morning, trying different routes each day. I belong to the Hash House Harriers, a walking club. When I walk with them, they speed me up. But when I walk alone, I have a tendency to slow down.

"And I like to travel. Last year, for my eightieth birthday, I drove back to the States and visited everybody on the West Coast who I correspond with at Christmas. I went to California, Oregon, Washington, and Missoula, Montana. I drove over 12,000 miles by myself. I purchased a new automobile so I didn't have to worry about car problems. I really enjoyed that trip."

"Wow! I wouldn't take on a trip like that alone even at my age. You're quite a woman."

She blushed. "I planned to fly this year, but it's so limiting, so I drove again—for 8,700 miles. My sister drove back with me, and we were waved right through the border. I think it's because I have Mexican plates and because of the Mexicans' respect for older people."

Virginia reached out to touch my hand. Her touch was

cool. A self-conscious grin accompanied a slight rise in her shoulders.

"You know, I like visiting my friends and family, but I am always anxious to come back home. In the States, everybody's so uptight and in a rush. I enjoy the slower pace here. I don't want to live like they do. I have to go back once a year for tax purposes; otherwise I wouldn't." She crossed her liver-spotted hands on the table in front of her.

"Do you travel much within Mexico?" I asked.

"Oh yes. Come late September or early October, when the waterfalls are flowing, I'm going to Copper Canyon. Mexico has so many beautiful places to visit."

"Do your family and friends visit you often?"

"My son is fifty-one. He'll never come to Mexico. When he was thirteen, we took our children to Puerto Peñasco on vacation because my husband likes to fish. My son couldn't understand such poverty existing. So he's never come to visit me. The sister who drove back with me last time visits every year. She loves it. My other sister and brother-in-law came once, but with no television in the guest condo, he was pretty bored."

"What advice would you give other women who are considering moving here?"

"My friend Alice is thinking of moving here. I said to her, 'Please come down and visit before deciding. There are definitely adjustments that need to be made.' She's unhappy with the U.S. government, but Mexico has its own share of governmental problems.

"You know, I think we all have friends who are very content to stay where they were born." I thought briefly of Liz and nodded in agreement. Virginia chuckled and continued. "In order to come here, I think they need gypsy blood. My father had it. If he hadn't had so many children—there were twelve of us—I think he would have drug us all over the country, getting a job here and a job there. I must have some of his gypsy blood running through my veins."

I smiled. "My kids always accused me of having gypsy

blood, too. It must be hereditary. My daughter has this same wanderlust."

"If it keeps getting more crowded here, I may move to the other side of the lake—if there's still a lake," she added.

I hoped the naysayers were wrong. Lake Chapala is the largest lake in Mexico—over sixty miles long—and is in jeopardy of disappearing. We had a very touching "Hands Around the Lake" event recently. Thousands of people, both Mexicans and gringos, came to the lake and encircled it with prayer and positive energy. Fox, the recently elected president of Mexico, had included saving the lake as part of his platform.

Virginia looked at her watch.

"We're almost finished, Virginia. Would you mind talking a minute about your health?"

"I'm pretty healthy. I go to an alternative-medicine doctor in Chapala. I don't believe in pills and prescriptions. For years I've had Medicare and a supplemental insurance policy in the States. I tried to sign up for IMSS, the Mexican national insurance, but was refused because I had skin cancer twenty years ago. If something really bad happens, I'll go to a VA hospital here, so why worry about it?"

"There's a VA hospital in Mexico?" I asked, slightly confused.

"No. But there's a military hospital in Guadalajara that honors our VA status."

Virginia picked up both our glasses and carried them to the sink. Looking out the kitchen window, she said, "Life's pretty good here for me. I've still got my health, I feel useful, and I'm doing the Lord's work."

I gathered my things and stood up. "And your love life?" I just had to toss that ball into the air, and she fielded it without a moment's hesitation.

"I'm eighty-one years old. I've taken care of one man and I'm not going to take care of another. I have a man friend. We go to dinner and on small trips together. But he's not moving in here. This is my time. We'll see each other on my terms."

So now I'd met my first octogenarian feminist.

Virginia walked me to the door, looked me right in the eyes, and asked, "Do you think my jealous husband, the fake ID, and recession in Japan were all part of the Lord's plan for me?"

16 Don't Back Up

*Life must be understood backward. But then one forgets the other clause—that it
must be lived forward.*
Soren Kierkegaard

Her hand went up to warn me. Through the chain-link fence,
our eyes met and BJ pointed to the ground. I followed her gaze
and gasped. Hundreds, maybe thousands, of gigantic black ants
were crossing the sidewalk between us —carrying trees. Okay, I
exaggerate, but very large pieces of trees.

"In one night, those guys devoured every flower and leaf
from one of my Japanese flowering trees," I said. "Three years
later, that poor tree is still dwarfed in comparison to its twin—
which they totally ignored."

"They're not getting past my gate. The gardener arrives
soon. He'll decimate those thieves." She offered her hand as
she opened the gate. "Hi, I'm BJ." Her grasp was firm and welcoming.

"Nice to meet you," I said, cautiously stepping over the
parade of ants. I perceived BJ to be a woman who was very
comfortable in her skin.

"Have you ever studied those ants?" I asked. She shook
her head. "One day, as I tanned by my friend's swimming pool,
I watched a procession of them hefting leaves ten times their

size and carrying them into a small hole in the ground. I put a stone over the hole, and before long, they had moved it and continued with their work. They're fascinating creatures."

"They're tree murderers!" she said with mock sternness.

We walked through the garden, shamrock green from the heavy August rains, into BJ's charming home in the village of San Antonio. As we high-stepped over hurdles of wire fences separating the living room from her small but adequate kitchen, two wire-haired dachshunds vied for our attention. "My puppy Katie isn't house-trained yet," she said with a shrug of her shoulders. "The wire fences keep her away from my good carpets. Franz is the larger one. They air freighted him to me from Frankfurt and I acquired Katie in Amsterdam a couple months ago." She picked up Katie, massaging her behind her ears, and then placed her on the floor. "Want some coffee?"

"Love some."

BJ walked to the counter. Dressed in a T-shirt, slim Wrangler jeans, and tennis shoes, she looked much younger than her seventy years. Her body was firm and gazellelike. Gentle wrinkles played around her gray-green eyes. I had the impression she was wise beyond, and young beneath, her years.

"I understand you show dogs," I said, eager to learn about BJ's life.

"Yep, about thirty years now. I started with smooth dachshunds and then switched to wire-haired. We used to hunt rabbits." She laughed at my shock. "We didn't shoot them and the dogs couldn't catch them. The dogs were judged by how well they track. It's a kick."

"You hunt down here?"

"No. I gave it up a few years ago. I can't chase the dogs anymore. It's hard enough to run after Franz when he gets through the gate. Once a dog is trained to hunt, as soon as he's off the leash, he's out of here." She propped Katie up on her hind legs. "I'm going to show Katie in puppy class at the dog show in Mexico City. If she gets her championship, I'll take her back to Holland and breed her. Cream and sugar?"

I shook my head. "Just black."

BJ sat down across the kitchen table from me and helped Katie back onto her lap. "I've had Franz for nine years. When my ex-husband took Duchess, our bitch, it was hard on both Franz and me. I wasn't sure how he would accept a new puppy. For the first few days Katie was here, he pretended she wasn't." She kissed Katie on the head and whispered, "But you won him over, didn't you?"

"This is a nice little house, BJ. Did you buy it?"

"No, no, no. I'd never buy a house here. I like being liquid. Besides, I'm getting too old for long-term investments." She grinned and poured tons of sugar and cream into her coffee. "This place costs me $300 a month on a five-year lease. Nacho, my landlord, lives next door. He's the town drunk and very colorful. He said to me when I moved in, 'Oh, *Señora*, if you have problems, just give me the words and I come over the wall for helping you.' "

"Have you had many problems?"

"Just one. I kept running out of water when I moved in. I have an underground water tank, my *aljibe*, and a pump. But the pump didn't work. It's supposed to move the water from the aljibe into the *tinaco*, a tank on the roof, and then gravity brings it down into the house. Nacho jury-rigged a fishing line, attaching it to the float in the tank on my roof and hung it outside my kitchen window. 'When you have no water,' he said, 'you pull this line and the pump brings water to your *tinaco*.' "

"Sounds like Mexican ingenuity," I said. "These guys can fix anything with spit, string, and glue. Of course it doesn't always stay fixed, but that's probably job security." Setting my cup in its saucer, I glanced around her home. The living and dining rooms were both adorned with oriental rugs and furniture that didn't appear to be made in Mexico. "You moved your furniture here?"

"Mm hmm. The move was a snap. First, I called North American Van Lines. They estimated the weight and volume and quoted me $7,500 from Dallas to Laredo. Mama mia, I thought, that's a lotta moola.

"I knew everything had to be changed to a Mexican truck

at the border, and the estimator told me they used Trans Container on the Mexican side. I called Trans and asked what they'd charge to ship my stuff from Laredo to Ajijic. $1,500. So I rented a U-haul and hired a few college guys to load it. The whole move cost me less than $2,000. Franz and I drove that twenty-eight-foot truck from Dallas, dropped it at the border, and Trans Container delivered my stuff three days later, as promised. *No problema.*"

"Ever drive a U-haul before?"

"Nope. I had a blast. The secret is to drive slow and don't back up."

"Is that one of your life rules?" I asked, sneaking a look at her from beneath my eyelashes.

BJ nearly choked on her coffee. "I guess it is. I have almost as much fun driving my yellow Beetle. I bought it as soon as I arrived. I laugh my head off driving it over the cobblestones. It rattles and I feel like I'm sixteen again."

"You're not afraid to drive here?"

"No. Not around the lakeside. I haven't worked up the courage to drive in Guadalajara, though." BJ smiled, as though relishing a private joke, and then said, "Soon after I got my Beetle, a local cop stopped me for going down the wrong way on a one-way road. I pointed to the arrow, which indicated one-way—my way. He told me it was the road I turned from where I had made my mistake. Then he opened his book and showed me that the fine was 300 pesos.

"I took forty pesos from my purse and held them in my lap. I'd been told to do this, although I'd never tried it before. 'No is possible for a receipt,' he said, 'but I forgive this time for forty pesos...and a kiss.' " BJ chuckled. "With a little quick math, I figured, Why not? My kiss was worth 260 pesos and good for a story or two. After he left, I was laughing so hard I could barely drive. I ran into a friend at the Lake Chapala Society and told her the story. She said, 'Oh, you met the kissing cop. Next time give him ten pesos and a big kiss. He's a great kisser.' "

"I've had my own run-in with the kissing cop," I told BJ.

"He took my license plates when I had parked on the wrong side of the street. In the end, he got fifty pesos and all I got was a hug. Where did I go wrong?" When we stopped laughing, I asked, "Do you worry about your car being stolen? I understand Beetles are hot items."

"No. I have a shut-off on the gas tank, I use a club device on the steering wheel, and I had an alarm system installed. It's practically thief-proof."

"May I look around?" I asked. BJ nodded and headed into the kitchen. I climbed over the makeshift kennel and wandered around the living room. Paintings of sailing vessels adorned each wall.

"You paint?" I asked, raising my voice so she could hear from the kitchen.

"I used to. But only to support my lust for ocean racing."

She returned to the living room, wiping her hands on a kitchen towel. "When I married in 1965," BJ explained, "my husband had retired from Wall Street. We bought a sixty-foot yacht and sailed for five years. I studied celestial navigation at the Hayden Planetarium. It was so much fun. I just adored Martin, but he was an alcoholic and a manic-depressive and finally we divorced. I still loved sailing, so I painted portraits of yachts, ships, and tugs for magazine covers, owners, and marketing brochures. It was a unique little niche and the money allowed me to continue racing."

"And you sailed down to Mexico?"

"No. After our divorce was finally settled, I moved to Dallas to be near my son, Brett. I tried to be a good grandmother, but I failed. His kids were spoiled rotten and triggered my spank reflex. I was afraid of child abuse laws. Since grandmothering wasn't my thing, I decided to head south. I'd been sailing on the east coast of Mexico many times, and when I was sixty, I returned with a backpack."

"Alone?"

BJ nodded. "Sure, why not?" She made my treks seem like milk toast.

BJ motioned me to take a seat on the sofa. "First of all,

I'm mad about the Mayan ruins. Second, I would never travel in a group. Even traveling as a couple, you miss so much because your attention is focused on each other. When I'm alone, I meet such interesting people—like Margaret." BJ leaned her head back on the sofa and continued talking with her eyes closed.

"I went from Belize up to Tikal. That involves a stay-over at Lake Elizabeth. The buses leave at three a.m. so people can get their chickens to the market. I met Margaret on this bus. Crippled from polio and about my son's age, she was backpacking to Canada by herself.

"They wouldn't let us take our melons over the border, so at the last rest stop, we sat at the edge of the road and ate them. I remember this fancy Land Rover with two older couples and a guide. They stopped when they saw us. 'Oh, you poor girls,' one woman cooed, 'are you all right?' I just looked at them with their curly silver hair and thought, God, I'm their age. We were having so much more fun than they were on their sanitized first-class hotel tour. It was a terrific moment. Margaret and I laughed, rubbed our sticky hands on our jeans, and climbed back into the sleazy bus."

"And your children," I asked, "what do they think of their gypsy mom?"

"My two daughters are both attorneys and we're not very close, but my son sat me down for an hour's lecture before I moved here. 'Mother,' he said, 'you don't look like you have a black belt in karate. I don't want you moving there by yourself.'

" 'Yes, Brett.'

" 'Mother, I don't want you riding on those Mexican buses. Everyone knows they go off cliffs.'

" 'Yes, Brett.'

" 'Mother, I don't want you buying a VW Beetle. It's unsafe. You're going to get killed in an accident.'

" 'Yes, Brett.'

"So of course I moved here, I take the buses, and I bought a Beetle." BJ slapped her hand on her knee. Her laugh came easily and reminded me of brass chimes tinkling in the breeze.

"My grown kids felt the same way," I said. "They wanted me to stay close by, but when I asked them if they promised to remain in the Bay Area if I stayed, they squirmed."

"And," BJ prompted, "did you ask them if they'd also fulfill your every need?" Now it was my turn to choke on the coffee.

We were a lot alike, BJ and I. I leaned back on the couch and said, "When I retired at fifty-one, I realized there would be no one in Silicon Valley to play with. Everyone my age was still working."

"That's why I'm here. Even in Scottsdale, where a lot of people are retired, Sun City West is filled with the most unadventurous, stick-in-the-mud people. They have nothing to do except find fault."

Playing devil's advocate, I prodded, "And the people down here?"

"They tend to reinvent themselves. We have an awful lot of colonels and generals—they've given themselves 'border promotions.' But so what? Maybe by rescripting their lives, they become more interesting people. I have a great neighbor and friend. She's a black lady who worked for the American Red Cross during World War II. On D-day plus ten, she drove an eighteen-wheeler onto Omaha beach. She is the widow of an ambassador to Kenya and was bringing medical equipment and supplies to the young soldiers who were wounded." BJ paused and stretched her arms above her head. "Where else would I meet such exciting people? Certainly not in Scottsdale."

Hoping to catch her off guard, I shifted position and looked directly into BJ's eyes, stifling a smile. "How's your love life, lady?"

Without missing a beat, she smiled broadly and said, "It's whatever I want it to be." Her timing was razor sharp. She waited until I was just ready to ask for an explanation and continued. "I'm not looking for any romance or any sex at this stage of my life. But I still like to flirt, so I date whomever I want. Since it's just casual dating, and I'm upfront about what I do and don't want in the relationship, I get to play the field without getting a bad reputation."

"Whom do you flirt with?" I asked.

"I've met a couple of nice men. They're about ten years younger…but who's counting?" BJ pushed her hair up off the back of her neck with both hands, cupping her elbows around her head. "I love my social life here. It's filled with interesting new friends, cocktail parties, and luncheons. I take Spanish lessons, and now that I'm settled and Franz has Katie, I'm going to start painting again. And then there are puppy kindergarten classes and gardening."

"I thought you had a gardener."

"I do, but I've forbidden him to clip anything. I think pruning is an art, like sculpting. Mexican gardeners let plants get so overgrown. You should've seen this place when I moved in. I added this brick patio and turned the jungle outside into my own Garden of Eden."

"I hate gardening," I said. "Last week, two of my green-thumb friends insisted we pull up my front rose garden and replant it. We shopped for colorful plants, brought in tons of dirt, and because I couldn't sit by while they did the work, I purchased a pair of garden gloves. 'Bugs and worms,' I told them, 'are not touching these hands.'"

"What did your gardener say?" BJ asked, obviously aware that Mexican gardeners have tender egos.

"He wanted to know if he'd been fired. I just smiled and said, 'No, *mi amiga* had an overwhelming urge to replant my garden. It would have been rude to deny her.'"

"Shall I put on another pot of coffee?"

"Not for me, thanks. No caffeine after eleven." BJ carried the empty cups and saucers into the kitchen, walking with an easy, confident stride. No way she's seventy, I thought.

"I forgot to tell you," BJ said when she returned. "I'm involved with the Daughters of the American Revolution and am fascinated with genealogy. There's a genealogy club at the Lake Chapala Society."

"What's the DAR like?"

"It's a bit boring, honestly. They do good works, but it's so political."

"Why do you belong?"

"My son wants his daughters to be Children of the American Revolution, and in order for that to happen, their grandmother needs to be an active member. Since I can't baby-sit, I figured this was the least I could do." I liked her unpretentiousness.

"BJ, why did you move to Mexico?"

"Adventure. Definitely adventure. I moved to Italy for two years when I was twenty-eight and studied art at the American Academy. I just cashed out and went. I didn't know a word of Italian, but was fluent by the time I left. Also, my ex-husband and I traveled extensively. We went on archeological digs in the Solomon Islands, and once we spent several months in the Amazon —where one of our staples was parrot stew."

"No! I used to own a parrot."

"Well, the plucking was colorful." I could tell from her grin she was baiting me.

"Gross!" I wrinkled my nose in disgust.

"It beats smoked monkey!"

My stomach did a flip-flop and I changed the subject. "How safe do you feel here in Mexico?"

"Safer than I did in Dallas or Belize. I got mugged once in Belize. The Mexicans are a gentle people. I don't hesitate to walk down to the restaurant alone or to the village plaza on Sunday evenings. I enjoy seeing the Mexicans all dressed up. The men and boys saunter around the plaza counterclockwise, and the women and girls stroll the opposite direction. It's their way of flirting. Older women sell little eggshells full of confetti, and when a young man takes a fancy to a young lady, he cracks the eggshell on her head, which crowns her hair with colorful scraps of tissue paper."

"And the girls are so shy."

"One of those Sunday nights, after I had returned home and was asleep, someone started fighting on my roof. Boom, scream, swat! I woke up momentarily, and thought, Interesting, and went back to sleep."

"How'd they get on your roof? And why weren't you terrified? They could have easily jumped down into your garden."

I was wising up to BJ's attempts to shock me. "Horses graze on the lot next door. It's easy to mount one, get up on the wall, and climb onto my roof. But they weren't after me, just a couple of drunks having it out with each other. Besides, people in this neighborhood call Franz muy bravo—very brave. He's taken a couple bites out of locals and word travels fast. Even the gardener won't work in the yard unless Franz is inside.

"In a small neighborhood like this, everyone knows everything and we all look out for each other. One day, after I had recovered from the flu, I walked down the street to get a pastry. The lady said, 'Oh, Señora, you are feeling better?' It makes me feel safe. I'd never want to live in a gated *gringo* community. Might as well be in Scottsdale then."

BJ tilted her head again and, with eyes full of mischief, asked, "Had enough?" I shook my head. "Okay, here's another great Nacho story. One night during martini number two, I was reading the paper and heard a knock on my inner door— the one in the garden. It's Nacho. He says, 'My wife, Manuela, is very bad woman. She calls police.' He begged me to hide him. My door was locked and I said, 'No, no man in my house.' Franz snarled and Nacho disappeared.

"A little later, my doorbell rang. I grabbed my flashlight and Franz followed me to the gate. There, by god, was Manuela, hands on her hips, with their eleven-year-old son and two policemen, each with a very big gun. They were looking for Nacho. I invited them into my yard and house. No Nacho. They eventually found him somewhere and put him in jail for the night. A few weeks later, Manuela moved out and Nacho's new girlfriend moved in."

"Why can't he manage both a wife and a mistress like most macho Mexican men?"

When we stopped laughing, I said, "It's been nearly a year since you headed south for adventure, BJ. Are you here for the long haul?"

"Until the lake goes dry. I love the water, and I can't tolerate Mexican beach towns because of the heat and humidity. There's a lake in Toluca that might be interesting. I'll check it out one day." BJ shrugged, her eyes twinkling. "After my five-year lease is up, who knows?"

17 | **Dancing Granny**

*Birds sing after a storm; why shouldn't people feel
as free to delight in whatever remains to them?*
Rose Kennedy

Turning right at the clinic, I drove slowly up a narrow cobble-stoned road with walled houses on either side. Number sixty-five—was that Chelsea's street number or her age? I wasn't sure. My electricity had been out for sixteen hours and only my computer knew the directions and her phone number. I tucked my car in as close to her gate as possible, hoping other traffic could squeeze by without scratching my Explorer, and smiled at the handful of cattle grazing behind a chicken wire fence next to her house.

As the front gate swung open, I found my eyes level with Chelsea's chin. Her long blonde pixie hairstyle framed a narrow face that sported a welcoming smile.

"Hi. Come on in." The breathless, little-girl quality of her voice contrasted sharply with the stately elegance of its owner. She wore a simple white knit shirt tucked into cranberry-colored shorts. I tried not to stare at her legs as I followed her inside. They seemed to go on forever.

"Ooh," I said. "I love your house. Who would've thought you could find something so nice in the middle of this neighborhood?"

Chelsea curtsied. "Thank you. I love it, too. I had wanted a two-bedroom home, but my friend insisted I come see this place." She spun around, taking it in with a grand sweep of her arm. "Who could resist? I love that the kitchen alcove is almost part of the living room. I walked in here, saw the kitchen, the telephone, the fan, a satellite dish, and a washer and dryer, and thought, Maybe I could sacrifice one bedroom."

Chelsea's hands and arms danced as she talked. Her slender fingers were tipped with white French fingernails, and three rings adorned each hand. I briefly wondered whether she had rings on her toes, too, but by then we were seated at the dining room table and I couldn't see. "And you have bóveda ceilings. Lucky you. Have you seen them built?"

"No, but they are stunning, aren't they?"

"When they extended my patio roof, I watched them being constructed. The workmen erected parallel steel beams about three feet apart, and then slightly arched a piece of plastic from beam to beam. The men sat on the steel beams and laid the bricks atop that arch. After they cemented between the bricks, they moved the plastic to the next section and repeated the process."

I scanned the living room. Displayed in glass-front cabinets, atop furniture, and tucked into alcoves were scores of teddy bears and dolls. "How long have you been collecting these?" I asked.

"Since my divorce, thirteen years ago—at the same time I took up ballroom and country western dancing. Seven nights a week I was on the dance floor somewhere." Chelsea drew circles on the table as though she were twirling her finger across the floor.

"How long were you married?"

"Twenty-eight years. We had three children."

"Where do they live?"

"Two live in Pittsburgh, where I lived most of my life, and one lives in Tucson."

"It must have been difficult, moving so far away."

"No, because at the time of my divorce, for whatever reason, my ex-husband turned my kids against me. When I needed them, they weren't there for me. I've visited my son once in Tucson, but I haven't seen my other son and daughter in thirteen years." My heart ached for Chelsea. I couldn't imagine not having a relationship with my children.

"Do you have grandchildren, too?"

She lowered her eyes. I bit my lip and wished I could have taken back my question.

"It broke my heart when my daughter took my two grandchildren away from me. They were the loves of my life. Both my sons have three children and one has an additional three stepchildren from his second marriage. Three of my eleven grandchildren I've never seen."

I waited.

She raised glistening eyes. "In Pittsburgh I did a lot of square dancing. Sometimes, after the dance we'd all go to a restaurant. All of a sudden tears would roll down my face and one of my friends would say, 'Okay, where's the little one?' There'd be some child nearby and I couldn't handle it." Chelsea straightened up in her chair and her voice strengthened. "That's when I figured it was time to leave Pittsburgh. Several fellow square dancers went to Tucson every winter. I thought, Why not? I retired in June of 1993 and left for Tucson in October."

"What kind of work had you done?" I wanted to move into less emotional territory.

"I did data-entry work for our consolidated financial statements. Our company was in real estate and venture capital."

"And you liked it in Tucson?"

"Oh yes." Chelsea's arms splayed out to the side like a kid welcoming her daddy home from work. "I loved it. I did plenty of square dancing and country western dancing. I hadn't planned on staying, but the weekend after Thanksgiving, I called my girlfriend in Pittsburgh." She balled her hand into a fist and punched the air in front of her. "I said, 'Put my house up for sale. I'm not coming home.' I never thought, What if? or Should I? I just knew it was where I wanted to stay. I bought a mobile home."

"Isn't Tucson awfully hot?"

"Yes, but not humid. My first year there, one hundred days topped 100 degrees."

I shuddered. "Too hot for me. You danced in that heat?"

"No. I danced at night. Besides, everything was air-conditioned. I had a real job during the day. I just can't sit still and do nothing, so I registered with a temp agency. During the weekdays I did data entry." Her fingers typed on the table, as though it were a keyboard. Chelsea's face became animated and she pointed at me with her forefinger. "Then one day I saw an ad for a hostess at Ventena Canyon, a five-star resort. I thought, Wouldn't that be fun? And it was. I could tell instantly whether or not I could jest with a customer or if they just wanted to be shown a table.

"One day, a short man came in. He was about five foot four." Chelsea held out her arm, indicating his head would reach up to her armpit if he were standing next to her. "He asked me, 'Chelsea, do you think I could have an extra cushion?' I said, 'Certainly,' and brought him one from the kitchen. He got up, added the cushion, and then wriggled back into his seat. I bent down, put my arm around his shoulder, and whispered into his ear, 'Do you think maybe a booster seat would help?' We both had a good belly laugh. My boss almost choked when I told him."

"Okay," I said. "Let me get this straight. You were retired but working full time during the day with the temp agency, and on the weekends at the resort, and dancing at night? I'm exhausted just thinking about it."

"But I was having fun. I love being involved with people."

"And then, after four years, you moved to Ajijic. How did that happen?"

"Well, I have an uncle who lives here, and I had come down many times for two- to three-week visits. And I stayed here for three months the summer before I moved down. By then I knew lots of people and could find my way around. I just thought, I think it's time to move to Ajijic. I rented this house in August but didn't move here until October. I had to sell the mobile home and handle a bunch of paperwork."

"What kind of stuff did you bring down with you?"

"Everything." She waved her arm inclusively around the house. "Except for the TV and the kitchen cabinets, everything is mine. I really worried if it would all fit." Chelsea's narrow mouth fascinated me. Perhaps she was English. "Well, it looks as though you selected everything especially for this house. You've created such a warm, inviting environment."

"Thank you. My landlord loves what I've done with it. He's so cute."

"How much rent do you pay?"

"Three hundred dollars. Can you believe that? And I've got a five-year lease."

"And what does it cost you to live here each month?"

"I'd say maybe $800, including rent." She slapped her hand on the table. "My Uncle Joe brags that he lives here on $500 a month. That's fine, but I get my nails done, my hair done, I buy clothes, and I eat out maybe once a day. I spend money. I can't just sit in this house every day and not do anything. I have a membership in the little theater." Chelsea gave me a curt little nod. "I spend my money."

I remembered my confusion about her house number and her age.

"How old are you, Chelsea?"

"Sixty-one." She leaned over and touched my arm. "I've never had a birthday party. Last year I said to my uncle, 'I'm going to have a big party when I turn sixty.' Well," Chelsea said with feigned indignation, "when I was recruited to dance in Broadway Babes at the little theater, my fellow dancers asked how I'd learned all those moves." Chelsea wiggled in her chair like a kid. "I told them I had danced with the Hot Flashes in Tucson, where you have to be either fifty or a grandmother. My friend Julie asked me, 'And which one of those are you?' Well, I said to Uncle Joe, proud as a peacock, 'If they don't believe I'm fifty, I'm sure as heck not going to have a sixtieth birthday party.' "

"Do you continue to dance here in Ajijic?"

"They don't have my kind of dancing down here. When I decided to move to Mexico, I thought, Well, I've spent fifteen years of my life dancing, now I want to do something else. I do a lot of volunteer work. I do bartending for a lot of fundraisers, for the music concerts and the chili cook-offs. She cocked her head to one side. "And I sold 15,000 pesos worth of raffle tickets for the mime show." She paused for my reaction and I gave her thumbs up. "Last year I was responsible for printing up the programs for The Little Theater. This year, I am director of the volunteers. I'm also responsible for handling the post-life-planning forms for the Lake Chapala Society (LCS)."

"How does that work?"

She rummaged through some papers on the table and pulled out a form, with a check stapled to it. "You complete this form, give me 200 pesos, and I get it notarized for you and give a copy to the funeral home."

"This form includes instructions for what you want done in case of death?" I asked, quickly perusing the questions.

Chelsea nodded. "If you die, the funeral home notifies the consulate, who notifies your family in the States or Canada. Sometimes when people sign the form, they say to me, 'Now I can die.' " We both laughed, although in reality it was not a laughing matter.

A short-haired cat sauntered into the dining room, stretching his body out to full length. "Did you bring your cat down with you?"

"No." Chelsea shook her head slowly from side to side. "I got her at the Humane Society. I hadn't planned on having one because there was no place here for a litter box. But six months after I'd moved in, I went to the Humane Society to meet a friend and see the kitties. This cat just kept rubbing my leg and purring. The woman at the desk said, 'She must know what's going to happen.' I asked, 'What's going to happen?' She said, 'Saturday, we're going to put her to sleep. She's been here five months.' Chelsea slapped her knees with both hands. "All of a sudden I found a place for the litter box."

"That was nice of you, Chelsea. You have a kind heart."

She nodded. "The first Christmas I was here, a friend asked me to play Mrs. Claus for a very poor neighborhood. He'd been involved building homes for these people who had been living in shacks. My friend and some other people collected toys and clothes for them throughout the year and gave them a nice Christmas. It was wonderful. The next year there weren't quite enough toys, so I broke out my two plastic garbage bags full of teddy bears. Those kids just broke my heart."

"Yes. I know what you mean. I volunteered at the orphanage for the first two years I was here, and as little as those kids have, they want to give back. At Christmas, we put on a party for them and gave presents to everyone. They also swung at several piñatas. As we said our farewells, several of the little ones came up and offered candies to us that they had saved from scrambling around on the ground after the piñatas burst. I didn't want to take them, because they have so little, but they really wanted to give something back. The Mexican children are very special and very unspoiled."

Chelsea stood up, a long way up, and stretched. "My first Christmas here, I put a manger scene out on my porch. The children in the neighborhood came in and looked at my decorations with their eyes like this." She made big circles around her eyes with her thumbs and forefingers. "Anyway, this little boy looked at the manger and then wagged his finger at me and scowled. '*Oh, no, Señora!*' He picked up the baby Jesus and handed him back to me."

"Why?"

Chelsea sat back down. "The Mexicans don't put the baby in the manger until Christmas Eve. This was the first of December."

"Oh, no! I've been doing it wrong for four years," I said. Noticing that only her front screen door was closed, I asked, "Do you feel safe here?"

"Completely. You know, I didn't find out until four

months ago that my landlord and all my neighbors are related. I don't bother shutting my doors or windows. I know my neighbors will look after me."

I grinned. "Speaking of neighbors, I saw cows grazing next door."

"Omigod. I go up in the morning and sit on the roof to watch them chase each other around. Do you want to see?"

I nodded and followed her past the living room, through her bedroom and out the door to the tiny staircase. Small white Christmas lights wound up the wrought-iron banister. "It's a mess," Chelsea said. "The windstorm last night knocked my roof trees over and broke the pots."

On the roof next door, a large dog slept peacefully in the sun. "He doesn't look like much of a guard dog," I said. Most of Mexico's roof dogs you'd never want to be within arm's reach of. They're trained to attack.

"Only a three-story-high, gray-green Christmas tree on the lot next door interrupted the lake view, and it took my breath away. "What kind of tree is that?" I asked.

"A Norwegian pine. Orchids climb up the center and when they bloom it's magnificent." I turned around to face the mountains. It amazed me how quickly they had turned green once the rainy season began. "See the horses there?" she asked. "The little one? He's just a few weeks old. When he was born he could hardly stand." Chelsea spread her feet apart and wobbled back and forth, mimicking the colt.

"They're building over there." She pointed to the west. "I think they've run out of money, though, because they stopped a few weeks ago." It never ceased to amaze me, the number of unfinished buildings in Mexico. Because interest rates are so high, there are no such things as building loans. When the people have a little money, they build a little more. *Poco á poco*. Bit by bit.

Chelsea tried to clear her throat. Her voice had been deteriorating during the interview. "I've a problem with my throat," she explained. "I think I had an allergic reaction to the anesthetic they gave me when I had my tummy tuck in February.

It's been like this since the day I left the hospital. Some days it's good and others it's all froggy and I start to lose my voice."

It surprised me that she mentioned her tummy tuck. No wonder her body looked so great—and here I was ready to sign up for dancing lessons. "Did you have it in Guadalajara? Were you happy with the job?" I asked.

"Yes to both questions. I've probably sent twenty people to my doctor. I paid only $1,000 and that included ten ultrasounds. I think I surprised the doctor. They operated on me Tuesday and the following Monday night I put on an evening gown and went to the theater. It was my night to greet people." Chelsea tossed her head and held her chin high. Folks at the theater asked me, 'What in the hell are you doing here?' I never took a pain pill. I hardly skipped a beat."

I shook my head. "That's not the same experience other friends of mine have had."

"Another thing. Everyone in that hospital is young and professional. The doctor spoke fluent English, but not the nurse. She was in my room every hour on the hour. We communicated through sign language. The medical care was excellent."

Looking down into her courtyard, I noticed hummingbirds fighting for their turn at the feeder. A gentle breeze wafted across the roof. "If it doesn't rain tonight, I'm going to have to water my flowers," She said.

"You've got a pretty nice life here, Chelsea. Do you have any regrets?"

"Heavens no." She chuckled. "My dad was bent out of shape when I moved here. He keeps waiting for me to say I've had enough and move back to Pittsburgh. And my friends laughed at me—especially since I don't do bugs. I have the exterminator come once a month. I've only seen three scorpions in the two years I've been here."

Chelsea took in a deep breath and shook her head. "I have no regrets and I wouldn't leave, because here I can save enough money to travel." Chelsea swooned. "I just came back from my dream vacation to London, Brussels, Liechtenstein,

Luxembourg, Innsbruck, Venice, Paris, and back to London. It lasted sixteen days.

"When I retired, I said to all my friends, 'My suitcase is always packed and wherever you go, I want to go with you.'"

18 | The Second Time Around

How a little love and good company improves a woman!
George Farquhar

A chestnut-skinned nurse met me at the white iron gate. "You are here to see Maxine?" she asked in broken English. She welcomed me with a broad smile and ushered me in.

I watched Maxine struggle across the lobby to greet me. She stopped momentarily, removing one hand from her walker to wave. "Hi, Blue. Come in, come in." Her cheery voice · matched her colorful outfit. A bright-pink blouse topped a mid-length black skirt. Around her neck she had tied a flowery scarf to add a touch of daffodil yellow. A raspberry-colored straw hat covered most of Maxine's wavy brown hair, which was threaded generously with gray.

Her five-foot-two stocky frame appeared sturdy in contrast to the reality of the chrome walker. I glanced at her feet. Thick legs with support hose disappeared into black orthopedic shoes. Maxine walked tall in her walker, carefully planting it in front of her and then taking a step to catch up.

After introducing me to several of the nurses and residents, Maxine said with pride, "I've lived here for two years and I love it." She turned to face the patio. "Aren't the grounds beautiful?"

Through the open glass doors, I saw several white wrought-iron benches dotting a large, well-landscaped yard, which overflowed with fruit trees and flowers. A pond and walkway invited residents and guests to stroll through and partake of its beauty. Two elderly men in wheelchairs talked about the upcoming Mexican election. Four women played a game of Hearts on the patio, protected from the hot midday sun by an umbrella.

"This is my room," Maxine said as we entered a small room off the hallway. It was simple—a single bed, a dresser, a table, and two easy chairs. A television was mounted in the corner next to a large window that looked out on the backyard. Maxine had made it home with fresh flowers, pictures of her family, and other mementos of her life.

"Let's talk outside," she suggested. "It's so beautiful today."

I smiled. "Just another beautiful day in paradise." She nodded. "Will we have enough privacy there?" I'd heard Maxine read several stories from her journal at the writers' club, and knew she held nothing back. Her honesty had startled me, and I found myself laughing, crying, and wriggling with embarrassment along with the rest of the audience.

"Privacy? I don't need privacy. My life is an open book. There are no secrets." Maxine touched my hand and said, "Come." She sat in a chair, her walker in front of her, and I took a place next to her so we could both enjoy the gardens.

"I turned seventy-nine last month," she said. "I've been a widow for two years."

That perplexed me. "I thought you said you had moved here alone."

"Yes, I did. I had been divorced thirty years when I moved to Guadalajara. I lived four years there and six years here at the Lakeside. I married after I moved to Mexico." She tapped her heart with her hand. "I'm an incurable romantic, as you'll soon discover."

A nurse brought us each a glass of lemonade. "Mmm," I cooed, as the cool liquid slid down my throat. "There's nothing like Mexican lemonade."

"They come right off that tree over there," Maxine said with a touch of pride in her voice. "We have fresh limones all year round."

"After being divorced thirty years, what brought you to Mexico?"

"First of all, I'll oversimplify the answer by saying 'adventure.' I had a wonderful life. I lived in San Francisco. I was a mediator for a law firm. I'd worked for them for twenty-three years, starting as a secretary. I have two daughters, and one lived close by. We talked every day on the phone and had a standing Saturday date.

"My daughter had a boyfriend from El Salvador. She's had many boyfriends, truth be told. On a trip back from El Salvador, they came through Mexico and she fell in love with the country. She started in on me. 'It's time you retired, Mom. Why don't you retire and move to Mexico?'

" 'I am not going to retire,' I told her. I was sixty-nine then, and I looked at all my friends who were retired. They were either sick or divorced or widowed, and I didn't want the life they led. They played bridge, they played other games, they met once a week and played poker. I don't like cards.

"One night these friends and I went to dinner. They all wanted separate checks and they started arguing. This one said, 'Oh, I didn't have coffee; you're the one who had the coffee.' The waiter stood in the corner laughing to himself, watching us old women quibble over fifty cents. I thought to myself, I'm not going to be like them. That night I went home, called my daughter, and said, 'I'm retiring and moving to Mexico.' "

"And you packed up and left?"

"No, it took me about a year. I researched the area and met the author of one of the books on retiring in Mexico—he lived only five minutes away from me. I thought I'd take Spanish classes, but I never got around to it." Maxine shrugged her shoulders and raised her eyes in mock embarrassment.

"My daughter and I took a look-see visit to Guadalajara for four weeks. We stayed at the Guadalajara Posada and spent a short time at the Lakeside. We'd been told by people at AMSOC [The American Society] in Guadalajara, 'Oh, don't go to the Lakeside because there's only a bunch of alcoholics there.'"

"So you decided Mexico was the place for you?"

"Yes, I decided to move to Guadalajara. I went home and gave notice at work. Of course I stayed long enough to train another person. I had a newly remodeled home in San Francisco. I'd recently bought everything new for it from top to bottom. I left everything in my house just as it was when I moved. That was my insurance policy, in case I didn't like it here. I came down and got a suite at the Guadalajara Posada."

"What were your first impressions?"

"All the people I met at the hotel were so friendly—the Jewish Americans, the Americans, and the Canadians. We all went out to breakfast my first morning there. Some of them had been there for years and showed me around the city.

"And the Mexican men—they liked me." Maxine took in a deep breath and swooned. I got a glimpse of the young woman still inside her. "I guess I've always liked men, and I think they knew it, because they treated me like a fifteen-year-old girl. I was seventy and I was never promiscuous. I was brought up in a small town near Providence, Rhode Island, and what you might call casual sex never appealed to me. I guess it was my romantic nature."

"You had a lot of dates?"

"A *lot* of dates—some with men twenty years younger than me. I carried around a few extra pounds and I couldn't speak the language, so I brought a book for translation. One time in a dark nightclub, my date used his cigarette lighter while I referred to my book. He got so mad he just threw the book on the floor. But we dated some more after that.

"He finally asked me if I'd be willing to take classes. He even offered to pay for them. I tried, but I had a mental block against learning languages."

Maxine loved telling her stories. Her raspy voice filled with joy as she rambled on about the details.

"Did you feel uncomfortable in Guadalajara without the language?"

"No, but I felt I was missing something. I was too lazy to learn, but I was too thrilled and excited and busy to let it stand in the way of my pleasure." That I'm-guilty-and-I-don't-care smile erupted again on Maxine's face.

"Was it easy to meet people?" I asked, hoping I'd have as much *joie de vivre* as she did when I reached her age.

"Yes, I've always had at least one real good girlfriend. It's a need I have to share things you don't share with the opposite sex. Just gossip and gab. Exchange ideas. I found that in Guadalajara. And after my husband and I got married, we had many couples as friends."

"Tell me about your husband."

"Abe was born in Colombia. His father had a lot of money. Abe had been married with seven children, but his wife, she was an alcoholic. So he divorced her. One of his daughters moved to Guadalajara and eventually he moved to Guadalajara to join her. He found an apartment two doors away from her."

Maxine smiled and ran her fingers lovingly across the bar of her walker. She was obviously remembering good times. "Serendipity," she said. "It was serendipity that we met. We met at the funeral of a mutual friend.

"I'd heard so much about this man Abe, who was renting an apartment in my friend's building. 'You should meet him, Maxine,' Gloria would say. 'His daughter has told me everything about him. You would not be meeting a stranger with untrue stories. He likes to cook and often brings meals over to me. You're both Jewish, although Abe came from Colombia.'" Maxine smiled broadly and added, "His parents came from Russia the same as mine did. He actually looked a lot like my uncle.

"But I'd just been burned badly by this gigolo I'd almost married. You heard my story at the writers' club, didn't you?" I nodded, remembering mostly that he was married and she didn't find out about it until she was almost the second wife.

"Well, I was going to be really cautious this next time.

"My friend's husband died, and at the funeral she pointed Abe out to me. 'Talk to him. He's a good man, Maxine.' Well," Maxine put both hands firmly on her walker and looked directly into my eyes. "I asked him two questions right off: 'Are you married?' and 'Do you have a girlfriend?' 'No,' he said, to both of my questions. Then I said to him, bold as ever, 'I want to be your friend.' I couldn't quite get the word *girlfriend* out of my mouth. And before he could say anything, I asked him, 'Do you want my phone number?'"

I chuckled out loud. "Pretty ballsy, I'd say."

Maxine laughed. "Well, I didn't have a lot of time left and it was as close to love at first sight as I'd ever been. I wasn't going to let him get away from me and I had never been like that before. Never ever. He was shy, so one of us had to do the asking."

I liked this woman's sass. Smiling, I asked, "How long before you got married?"

"Four months. He asked me to live with him first, and I said, 'No, I'm not that kind of girl. My daughter does it, but it's not for me. I want to be married.' So he asks, will I go away with him for a weekend? 'Sure,' I say, 'why not?'

"So, my Abe, he's a very cautious man and he says, 'We should get blood tests.' I should've thought about that myself. There were twenty-five possible tests we could take. We took all of them. I passed with flying colors. Okay, maybe I could have lost twenty pounds, but who's counting? Neither of us had AIDS. I'm sure that's what he wanted to find out about. Abe, he had high blood pressure but otherwise was very healthy."

"The sex that weekend...it was terrific." Maxine looked at me and laughed. "You're not shocked, are you?" I shook my head, but I was a bit surprised.

"'So, why wait?' he said. We got married in Las Vegas. We flew to San Francisco and sold my house, kit and caboodle, and that ended my insurance policy. His youngest son and my youngest daughter were there. His son asked me privately, 'Will you take care of my father?' You know, I did that, and at Abe's funeral, all seven of his children cried and thanked me for taking care of him. We were married six years—six good years. I miss him a lot."

I wondered if she would start crying. Not Maxine. She seemed so full of life. I couldn't imagine her spending too much time grieving. "Did you move to the Lakeside after Abe died?" The sun crept in between the branches of the trees, and I put on my sunglasses.

"Oh no, we moved to Chapala about five years ago. It was hard leaving his daughter and grandkids, but several of our friends had moved here and we found out there were wonderful people here. They weren't all alcoholics!"

A bell chimed. "That's the fifteen-minute signal for *comida*. We eat a big meal at 2 p.m. and then just a snack at night. The food's really delicious here. As good as in a restaurant."

"Well then, Maxine, in our last fifteen minutes, please tell me how you ended up at this nursing home."

"It's a nursing *and* retirement home. Some folks need more care than others. I don't need care, but I do need company. I don't like living alone. If I could just get rid of this walker, I could probably find a man, but who wants to live with someone who has to drag this dratted thing around?"

She picked up the walker and banged it on the ground.

"How did this happen?" I asked.

"I fell down at a dance and fractured my hip. Then I had surgery through the IMSS social medical system to replace part of my hip. The surgeon screwed up and left me in a lot of pain. They had put the prosthesis in the wrong place. It didn't show up on any X-rays. Can you believe that? If I'd been in the States, I'd have been a millionaire through lawsuits. Finally, I found another orthopedic specialist in Guadalajara. He'd asked me to do a lot of physical therapy before he performed the second operation.

"Irresponsible me. Because I was busy, I didn't do what I'd been told. Arthritis set in, and there wasn't enough of a socket left to fully hold the prosthesis in the second operation.

Three weeks after that second operation, it just came out. The doctor said I had to make some tough choices.

"Of course I had this walker by then. He told me my knees were eventually going to need surgery. If the third operation was successful and I walked with even just a cane, the pressure on my knees would get stronger and within four to six months I'd need surgery on both knees. He looked me right in the eye and said, 'These operations are not always successful for people your age. You might be in a wheelchair for the rest of your life.' "

"That was just a few weeks before my husband got really sick. He died of congestive heart failure."

Maxine sighed. Her shoulders slumped and some of the color had drained from her face. "Anyway," she took a deep breath and let it out slowly, "you wanted to know how I ended up at this home. I've explained the walker, but not the home. Gloria, who I knew very well since I moved to Guadalajara, she called me one day and asked me, had I ever heard of a person named Monica?' I had. 'Call her,' she said." Maxine turned to look into the lobby and explained, "Monica manages this home."

Maxine sat up straighter and a joyful smile spread across her face. "I want you to meet her. She's young, she's beautiful, and she's intelligent. She is so loving and so wonderful. It's because of her that I love it here. She takes us everywhere—even to Guadalajara. I lunch with friends in town two to three times a week.

"I still go out dancing, as long as my walker is within arm's reach. And I watch Monica do line dancing twice a week. Of course, you know I write, and I also read and teach English to some of the workers here at the home. It just doesn't seem like there's enough time in the day to do everything I want to.

"I didn't want to live alone after Abe died. My kids wanted me to move back to the States, but I didn't want to. I'm here, first of all, because I love living in Mexico. Second, because I love Monica, and I have a couple of good friends who live in the Lakeside area. And my husband's daughter and the grandchildren are close by in Guadalajara.

"I can't see paying three or four times what I pay here to stay in some stuffy retirement home in the States with 140 residents and people who don't care about you. No, that's not for me."

Maxine looked at me and sighed. A half smile played at her lips. "What I really want is a man in my life. Sex is not the first factor, or the second, or the third. I want someone looking after me. Sharing. Partnership. This is very important. Until I find him, this retirement home is the next best thing for me."

Postscript:

Nearly one year after this interview, Maxine passed away at the nursing home. Her high energy, humor, and uplifting spirit are missed in this community.

19 | **Search for Serenity**

*I live not in myself, but I become
Portion of that around me: and to me
High mountains are a feeling, but the hum
Of human cities torture.*
George Noel Gordon, Lord Byron

When I had asked for this interview; Diane invited me first for a bowl of homemade vegetable soup. Coupled with bread fresh from the bakery, a glass of iced tea, and cookies, it was a feast.

Diane's eclectic courtyard home reflected her Hispanic tastes and was filled with treasures from all parts of Mexico— masks and dolls, pottery and plants, and a miniature *castillo* I coveted. *Castillos* are complex thirty-foot-high bamboo edifices erected for launching fantastic fireworks displays during Mexican fiestas.

After eating, we each relaxed on one of her two sofas. Diane wore her beautiful gray hair cropped short. Bushy black eyebrows tented deep brown eyes framed with wire-rim glasses. A loose, sleeveless sundress camouflaged what I imagined was a nice figure. "Okay, Diane, I want to know how a nice Jewish gal from the big city of New York found her way to this small cobblestone village of Ajijic."

"I had no plans to retire. I was in love with my job and

figured I'd work until I was sixty-five. I lived on the Upper West Side of Manhattan, working as a teacher and child guidance counselor. I loved New York's energy and excitement, its hustle and bustle. But when the funding started to disappear from the support agencies I referred my kids to, it stopped being fun. I felt impotent. I gradually become aware of an increased sense of dissatisfaction."

The combination of her heavy New York accent and wide, expressive mouth fascinated me. "How old are you now?"

"Fifty-eight. I lived in New York for thirty years."

"So frustration with your career prompted you to move to Mexico?"

"No. Other parts of my life were also coming to a natural closure. I let myself get involved—like head-over-heels-in-love involved—with a married man. His marriage was an unhappy one, but I knew he wasn't going to leave his wife. We worked together, and each day was an emotional roller-coaster ride for me." She paused to light up a cigarette and check my reaction.

"Sure, I know the statistics and the downside of getting involved with a married man, but I believe that affair was important to me because it made me question why I was willing to risk my comfortable relationship with Len. And deep inside I realized both Len and I knew our twenty-year relationship had run its course."

"So it was the affair that made you decide to leave New York?" I asked. I knew I'd get my answer sooner or later.

"No. I experienced this growing need for change more as an unfolding than any single event."

Diane tilted her head, apparently thinking through the chain of events. A small white poodle with pink ribbons on her ears jumped onto the couch next to her. "Three years ago the Board of Education offered me a great early retirement package. It was then that I took a good hard look at my life and myself. I'm a great believer in synchronicity, and it seemed like neon signs were flashing into my living room window: 'It's time to move on, Diane. It's time to move on.'

"I knew I needed to leave New York City, but at the time

I had no idea where to go. I'd given some thought to upstate New York. It's beautiful there, but so cold in the winter. And it's expensive. I'd never owned a house or a car and hadn't built up a nest egg. I worried about 'expensive' and 'inflation' on a fixed retirement income."

I looked around her home. She had most of the creature comforts one could ask for. I made a mental note to return to her finances later in the interview.

"Several years earlier, I had started researching retirement options. I'm a packrat, and after some searching, I found one particular book I was looking for, extolling the joys of retiring in Mexico. It still sounded good to me, so I talked my friend Judy into going with me to Guadalajara for a short vacation."

"Why did you choose this part of Mexico?"

"Originally, I thought I wanted to live in Guadalajara, because I was a city girl; but we visited Ajijic first and never made it any further. Ajijic felt to me like a healing place. It had what I needed to be happy. There was an international airport and a big city close by."

Diane leaned forward, elbows on her knees. "Even though I speak almost fluent Spanish, I wanted to live in or near an English-speaking community. I wanted homeopathic doctors and a spiritual center. Although I'm Jewish by heritage and culture, my religion is more aligned with New Age philosophies, and I wanted friends who held similar beliefs."

A large gangly dog leapt into her lap. The poodle sneered at him and, like the lady she was, moved aside to give the intruder enough space. "Chuy's still an overgrown puppy," Diane explained, "a big, rambunctious one." She snuffed out her cigarette and scratched Chuy's belly. "Chica just tolerates him.

"When we first got to Ajijic and walked down the main street, I said to Judy, 'This place looks dumpy.' Buildings were run-down and there was garbage in the gutters. I'd been prepared for a beautiful artists' colony. But the people—both the Mexicans and the Northerners—were wonderful. We met several couples who invited us into their homes, gave us information on costs, places to go, and who to talk with. We felt like they'd taken us into their family.

"Later, as we walked around town, I was awed by the fragrant flowers. We started peeking behind the bedraggled gates into glorious gardens and stunning homes. We strolled along the lake, spoke to the fishermen, and marveled at the large white egrets. The next morning, we were awakened by the sounds of birds and roosters and the clip-clop of horses on the cobblestone roads. I was smitten. I knew I belonged to this place, or maybe it belonged to me."

I understood exactly what Diane meant. After three days in Ajijic I felt that perhaps I had lived here in a previous life. The calling was strong—not in any rational way, in some deep unexplored part of me. Maybe it's just that in the beauty of this area and in the quiet, we can listen more easily to ourselves.

"On Sunday, we discovered a place called New Dimensions. It's a New Age nondenominational spiritual center. Ajijic also offered several types of yoga classes, three or four gyms, local homeopathic doctors, and health stores. The friends, of course, I'd need to wait for, but I knew it would be easy to meet people who shared my interests and beliefs.

"After two weeks, I felt like a new person. Refreshed. Cleansed. It's funny, but after so many years in New York City, I wasn't even aware how hectic my life had become. I was in the middle of it every day and so was everyone else. Such a simple little truth I had found. It wasn't necessary or even normal to be surrounded by people rushing, by rude people. Here, I didn't have to be continuously on my guard. No traffic and no sirens. What I loved most was the serenity and peacefulness, the sounds of the birds and the smells of the flowers.

"At some level in my own consciousness, I knew this prescription was just what the doctor ordered. It was a deeply personal awakening and something I couldn't even talk to Judy about."

An evening breeze whipped through the living room and Diane got up to fasten the screen door leading to the courtyard. Chuy followed at her heels. "So," I prompted, when the two were comfortably cuddled up again, "you were moonstruck?"

"Yes, but not ready to chuck it all. A couple months later, I came back to spend some time by myself. That feeling of belonging was still there.

"When I got home, I accepted the Board's retirement offer and ended my affair with Max. Len and I parted on good terms. When the taxi came to pick me up, we cried, held each other, and then we closed that door. I was putting an exciting affair, a thirty-year career, and a twenty-year relationship behind me. I felt lonely, confused, euphoric, and apprehensive all at the same time.

"My family thought I was a little crazy—no, a lot crazy. Of course they had their preconceived ideas of what Mexico was like, even though they'd never been here. But my two best friends, Susan and Judy, supported me. 'Do what will make you happy,' they said. 'Go for it.'

"Susan bought a computer so we could e-mail each other daily. Judy and Susan helped me sort, pack, and get rid of things. I remember Judy shaking her head as she looked at the stacks and boxes waiting for a pickup from Goodwill. 'How can you give up your things?' she asked. 'I never could.'

" 'It's just stuff,' I said. 'I want a new life and new things.' My laptop, printer, and modem fit in my carry-on, and as long as I had those, the rest was either replaceable or unnecessary. Who needs heavy winter coats and knee-high boots in Mexico?"

My friend Liz and I had had this same discussion before I left. She was aghast at my garage sale. I was selling most everything—even things that she and my kids had given me as gifts. 'May I take these back if you don't want them?' she asked. I felt bad, but like Diane, I wanted to start over. I'm trying very hard not to accumulate more things that will need to be sold in another garage sale.

"But what about the big city, Diane? The culture? Don't you miss that at all?"

"Susan also asked me if I'd miss the culture and the diverse activities of New York City. As I thought about her question I realized that although I'd been in the middle of it, most of it hadn't been within my grasp on a teacher's salary.

" 'Nope,' I answered. 'But I might miss the restaurants and shopping. I'm sure I won't be able to call a deli at three a.m. and order a Rueben sandwich delivered or walk down to a corner sushi bar.' "

"Hey," I said, "we have a sushi bar here now and they just started a taxi delivery service for restaurants, so maybe you can get your Reuben sandwich delivered—just not at three a.m."

Diane laughed and walked over to the stereo to turn some background music on. When she returned to the sofa, she continued. "The move was so much easier than I expected. A friend I had made during my vacation met me at the airport with six bags that held the remnants of my New York life. She had found a house for me to rent. I sent her a deposit, sight unseen. Located close to the plaza, it was fully furnished, with two bedrooms and two baths for $500 a month.

"It's the New Yorker in me, I guess, who likes the security of living downtown and having neighbors watch over me. The house reeked of authentic Mexican. I put my office upstairs next to a large open balcony so I could see the mountains, lake, and streets, and listen to the vendors and musicians.

"There was a big thunderstorm the first week and the power went out. I ate my dinner by candlelight under an umbrella of lightning, listening to the applause of thunder. It was another sign for me I had made a good choice. I knew this house and neighborhood would bless me." Diane sighed and nuzzled her chin into Chuy's neck.

I turned around at some noises in the kitchen.

"That's Juanita, my maid. The first week I was here I found her. She's been my indispensable maid and friend since then. She fusses over me like I was one of her brood. She does the laundry, ironing, cleaning, and shopping. She even doctors me with herbs when I'm sick. Juanita comes six days a week, and my gardener three times. I pamper myself with a weekly massage, manicure, and pedicure. I'd never have considered myself a princess in New York, but sometimes down here, it feels pretty close."

Before the interview, I had warned Diane about some of my questions being personal and expressed my hope she'd be willing to share her financial situation with me. "Now is the time," I said, "for the money stuff. How much does it cost you to live here?"

Diane pushed Chuy away, sat up, lit a cigarette, and inhaled deeply. I could tell this was uncomfortable for her.

"With all my entertainment, little luxuries, utilities, phone, and auto expenses plus insurance for car and house, and eating out about 80 percent of the time, in addition to rent, I probably spend $1,500 per month. I never want for anything, including travel throughout Mexico and trips back to the States. Although if I were totally selfish, I'd stay here and make everyone come visit me!

"In Guadalajara, I've been able to enjoy so much more culture than in New York. Front-row seats for the Jalisco or Philadelphia Philharmonic orchestras cost less than ten dollars. Operas, ballets, and symphonies from all over the world come to the city. I joined our Music Appreciation Club because we get group rates and bus rides to Guadalajara for special events.

"In addition to the cultural activities, I take yoga, French, self-defense, and art classes. Some of my favorite things to do are free. I spend time on my computer, read, work in the garden, walk my dogs along the lake, and visit with friends. I really enjoy the local Mexican fiestas and it seems like there's always something happening. The best part is, with our beautiful weather, I can do most everything outdoors, year-round." Diane turned around to look outside the window at her courtyard. "Every morning I go outside and say, 'Thank you, Lord, for letting me live here.' "

I chuckled. "I guess this more than makes up for being deprived of Rueben sandwiches at three in the morning, huh?"

Diane stretched out her arms above her head and smiled. "No, compared to New York City, I don't feel deprived; I feel blessed. It's been almost four years now. It doesn't seem possible. I have many wonderful friends among the Northerners and a few in the Mexican community. I've attended Mexican weddings, baptisms, and christenings and occasionally been invited into their homes." Diane leaned back and exhaled slowly. "In spite of my fluency in Spanish and my familiarity with the Latino culture, I'm still trying to understand some of the subtle cultural differences. I know it will take many years, maybe many lifetimes, to truly understand the nuances of another culture. After all, it's taken centuries to develop it."

Chica stretched out her legs and decided it was her turn for attention. Her manner and regal bearing made me wonder if she wasn't really a cat in dog's fur. As she maneuvered her way onto Diane's lap, Chuy decided I was a good second choice and plopped up next to me. "Did you bring the dogs with you?" I asked.

"Dogs in New York? No, I've never owned pets before. I adopted these two about five months ago. I hoped they'd bark if strangers were around, but they don't. Fortunately, we've fallen madly in love with each other and I can't imagine my life without them. Juanita stays with them if I want to travel, so I don't feel tied down."

Diane picked up Chica and rubbed noses with her before continuing. "I've discovered these dogs are teachers for me—teachers of patience, selflessness, and unconditional love. Besides patience, which is something everyone who moves here must learn, I think part of my healing process is getting to know myself better and learning to enjoy my own company.

"It's amazing, but after a twenty-year relationship, I don't feel I need a partner to be happy. I've found great women friends. We accept each other for who we are and we can be ourselves. So I'm really happy. I'm financially comfortable. I'm healthy and my environment is beautiful. If I meet somebody special now, it would be icing on the cake."

Diane removed her glasses and cleaned them with the bottom of her sundress. Her voice softened as she continued to caress Chica. "In New York, I wasn't aware of the continual high stress I was under until I came to this peaceful, quiet village. Here, I don't feel the need to be on a fast track. The contrast has smacked me in the face.

"My body thanks me for the lack of tension and slower pace. In some mysterious way, I think this is what I've been looking for a long time, but didn't know it—a kind of serendipity. I'm more mellow now and not as impatient or judgmental. I'm more in touch with my spiritual nature. The beauty of this place continually delights and astounds me.

"I'm definitely happier in Mexico; and what's more important, I like *me* better now."

Postscript:

Two years later, Diane celebrated her sixtieth birthday with a street party. About 200 people attended. Half were Mexican; half were gringos. She had a two-story-high castillo *erected in an empty lot across the street from her. She furnished food, drinks, and music as a way of giving back to the community some of the joy she has received living in this beautiful land. Six months later, Diane purchased her very first home in the village of Ajijic.*

About the Author

Karen Blue, known by friends as "Blue," chucked corporate life in 1996 at age 52 to live and write in Ajijic, Mexico. She has published several articles in English language newspapers and authors a monthly column on Mexico's largest Internet site, titled "Living in Mexico—From a Woman's Perspective" at *http://mexconnect.com/mex_/travel/blue/askblue.html*

In the late eighties, she co-founded both the Silicon Valley and San Francisco chapters of the national Association of Women Business Owners.

Blue holds a BA in Business Management. She held several corporate management and consulting jobs in Silicon Valley in both business-to-business marketing and international customer service organizations.

She has two grown children and two young dogs. Her days are spent enjoying the beautiful weather of the Lake Chapala region, making soft-sculptured dolls, writing a novel—*Leap Into Life*—traveling, and marketing *Midlife Mavericks*.

She also plays bridge, Scrabble, Mah Jongg, Pinochle, and Cranium when she can hogtie people into joining her.

Blue welcomes comments and questions. She can be reached by email at: *mexicoblue@prodigy.net.mx*. Visit her website at: *www.mexicoblue.homestead.com*.

Quick Order Form

Fax orders: Send this form.
 In the U.S: 954-755-4059   In Mexico: 013-766-2210
Phone Orders:
In the U.S. only: 800-636-8329
Web orders: http://www.upublish.com/books/blue.htm

(Or, at major on-line bookstores. You receive the books faster if
you order direct from the publisher and I get twice the royalty)

Name: _____

Address: _____

City: _____ State/Prov: _____

Zip Code _____ Country: _____

Day Telephone: _____ Night Telephone: _____

E-mail address: _____

Order Information:
Please send me _____ copies of *Midlife Mavericks: Women
reinventing their lives in Mexico*, by Karen Blue. Paperback.
ISBN No: 1-58112-719-7

List Price: **$19.95** each, plus airmail shipping and handling to the
U.S., Canada and Mexico [$4.90 for first book and $1.95 for each
additional book] Florida residents please add 6% sales tax.

Payment Information: Circle One:
Check   Visa   Master Card   American Express   Discover

Card Number: _____

Name on Card: _____ Exp. Date: _____

Total Price: _____

Comments: